THEY WENT BROKE?!

Bankruptcies and Money Disasters of the Rich & Famous

THEY WENT BROKE?!

Bankruptcies and Money Disasters of the Rich & Famous

ROLAND GARY JONES, ESQ.

GRAMERCY BOOKS
New York

This 2002 edition is published by Gramercy Books, an imprint of Random House Value Publishing, Inc., 280 Park Avenue, New York, NY 10017, by arrangement with Roland Gary Jones.

Gramercy is a registered trademark and the colophon is a trademark of Random House, Inc.

Printed in the United States of America

Book design by Christine Kell

Random House
New York • Toronto • London • Sydney • Auckland
www.randomhouse.com

A catalog record for this title is available from the Library of Congress

ISBN: 0-517-22012-1

9 8 7 6 5 4 3 2 1

CONTENTS

$$$

Heroes and Villains

$ $ $

Patriots

$ $ $

Politicians

$ $ $

Celebrities

$ $ $

Musicians

viii

$ $ $

Artists and Writers

$ $ $
Actors

$ $ $

Sports Stars

$ $ $

Inventors

$$$
Moguls

FOREWORD

I am writing this book primarily because I need the money to pay creditors.

If you're the average reader, you're also strapped to the gills. In the year 2000, during boom times, more than 1.2 million people filed for bankruptcy—the largest number since the bankruptcy laws were written. In 2001, even more found themselves in bankruptcy court. I have met some of these people because I am a bankruptcy lawyer.

What has struck me most while practicing my profession is the emotional pain people go through when filing for bankruptcy. I hope this book lessens that pain.

Bankruptcy hurts because we view it as a personal failure with an added dose of guilt. We see it as involuntary stealing. Of course, no creditor would dispute that take on things. But the people I write about (excepting the clearly felonious) are amongst the world's most admired figures. No one (except their creditors) would characterize Thomas Jefferson or Rembrandt Von Rijn as thieves. Yet both died owing a fortune.

Anyone can wind up bankrupt, whether you're saint (Cotton Mather) or spy (Ronald Pelton), painter (James McNeill Whistler) or president (Ulysses S. Grant). And people go bankrupt for a thousand different reasons. You can go bankrupt because a big investment goes sour (Wayne Newton) or because your partners rip you off (Vic Damone) or because you get hurt in a freak car accident (Margot Kidder).

Bankruptcy is like cancer. It can strike anyone and no one really knows why or how to predict it. Like cancer, once you owe enough money and the interest is accruing, there's often nothing you can do about it. The point of all this is to feel a little more compassion for people in financial trouble, and most importantly, for yourself.

Roland Gary Jones
January 31, 2001
New York City

DEDICATION

To my wife, Nance; my daughter, Katherine; my brother, Clark; my father, Daniel; and to the memory of my mother, Elyane.

Also dedicated to all my clients and the judges and the entire support staff at the Southern and Eastern Bankruptcy Courts of New York who have put up with me over the years.

HEROES &
VILLIANS

$ $ $

Francis Bacon
BRITISH STATESMAN AND PHILOSOPHER

Francis Bacon was the son of Nicolas Bacon, the Lord Keeper of the Seal of Elizabeth I. Since he was the youngest son, he got nothing when his father died. Constantly in debt, he was arrested and thrown into debtors' prison in London Tower for an unpaid account with a local merchant.

While he eventually rose to become Lord Chancellor of England, his financial problems continued to dog him. Late in life, Bacon took bribes as a judge and was again locked up in the Tower. He never again held public office and, when released, retired to focus on philosophy.

$$$

Horatio William Bottomley
BRITISH CON MAN

Horatio Bottomley published John Bull, a World War I weekly that hyped rabid patriotism. He also sold millions of war bonds, ostensibly to finance the war. Actually, while the boys he was "financing" were getting massacred due to lack of supplies, Bottomley was blowing the money on racehorses, hotel suites and high-class hookers.

The British cast him into jail. He died bankrupt.

$$$

Bob Brennan
STOCK SWINDLER

Brennan was famous for his TV commercials depicting him stepping out of a helicopter. A notorious penny-stock promoter, he filed Chapter 11 after judge found that he had defrauded investors. Brennan was later indicted for bankruptcy fraud because he allegedly tried to hide $500,000 in gambling winnings during his personal bankruptcy case.

$ $ $

John Brown
ANTI-SLAVERY HERO

Herman Melville called him "the meteor of the Civil War." John Brown tried to start a slave rebellion by raiding a Virginia weapons armory at Harper's Ferry and turning the weapons over to slaves.

The scheme failed and he surrendered to Union forces. Outraged by Northern support for a man that tried to get Southern whites butchered, Southern states withdrew from the Union. If one man could be held responsible for starting the Civil War, that man was John Brown.

Before Brown got political he failed as a real estate speculator. Brown filed for bankruptcy in 1842 under the spanking new bankruptcy laws. He had lost all his property by speculating on Ohio real estate values. Brown had bought property in the town of Franklin Mills, which he heard would be a railroad station. Unfortunately, the railroads bypassed the town.

A frustrated and angry Brown looked for something else to do. He found it at Harper's Ferry.

$$$

George Catham
BRITISH THIEF

George Catham, the legendary cat burglar and model for the Peter Sellers film, *The Pink Panther*, crept away with some $100 million in jewels. Catham's Achilles heel was gambling. He lost it all, leaving a casino at Monte Carlo the final beneficiary of his record-breaking larceny.

$$$

Dr. Denton Cooley
FIRST U.S. HEART TRANSPLANT SURGEON

As of the early 1990s, Dr. Denton Cooley performed more than 80,000 heart surgeries. He was also the first American to do a heart transplant and the first surgeon anywhere to implant an artificial heart.

His leveraged real estate investments crashed when the Houston economy suffered from the drop in oil prices. When he filed for Chapter 11 bankruptcy protection he owed 200 creditors over $97 million.

The Chapter 11 plan allowed him to retain most of his $9.7 million annual salary. He bought back two Galveston beach houses and two Rolls-Royces from his bankruptcy estate.

$ $ $

Henri Dunant

FOUNDER OF THE INTERNATIONAL COMMITTEE OF THE RED CROSS

Henri Dunant devoted his life to starting the Red Cross after he witnessed firsthand the massacre of 40,000 Austrian and French troops during the Battle of Solferino. He financed the fledgling organization's meetings by hitting up friends and family. When that money ran out, Dunant turned to quick money deals. One of these schemes involved an investment in an Algerian marble quarry located near the town of Felfela, between Philippeville and Bona. He financed this gamble with high-risk securities trading on the Paris stock market. Dunant also got himself appointed a director of Credit Genevois, a shaky Paris bank.

The bank apparently made a huge loan to the Dunant-owned quarry. After the quarry failed, the bank collapsed and the Swiss Court of Civil Justice went looking for a scapegoat. They found Dunant guilty of fraud and double-dealing. Dunant became personally liable for all the bank's losses—an insurmountable liability.

Ruined both financially and in the press, Dunant resigned under pressure his post as secretary of the Red Cross. He fled Geneva and spent his remaining days roaming Europe as a penniless vagabond.

$ $ $

Lord Elgin
BRITISH PHILANTHROPIST

Lord Elgin was a nineteenth-century British ambassador to Turkey. Looking to decorate his Scottish palace, he got permission to copy the famous sculptures of the Greek Parthenon. Bored with copies, Elgin had work crews with giant saws hack the sculptures off the Parthenon during the night.

But Elgin forgot to figure out how to pay the huge costs of shipping all that marble all the way back to England. Faced without enough funds to pay the Victorian-era Teamsters, he fenced the stolen art to the British government. Still unable to pay debts, Elgin fled the country to escape debtors' prison.

Things got worse. While he was hiding out, a mysterious disease rotted away his nose, leaving a disgusting gash. Realizing at last that Elgin was a serious loser, his wife ran off with his best friend, Robert Fergusson. Elgin finally died bankrupt and very weird looking in 1841.

$ $ $

Heidi Fleiss
HOLLYWOOD MADAM

Heidi Fleiss, the infamous Hollywood Madam for the rich and famous, filed a Chapter 7 case in December 1999. Fleiss, who once made thousands of dollars a day satiating sexual appetites, listed assets of only $5,000 in jewelry and an unglamorous $200 in clothing.

Turned in by a boyfriend, she spent the years 1997 to 1999 in prison for tax evasion, money laundering and attempted pandering. Fleiss's bankruptcy wiped out credit card debts of almost $270,000 and an $85,000 back-rent debt from her failed Santa Monica under-wear business, Heidi Wear, Inc.

Finally, Fleiss did to her lawyers, the old-line firm of Gibson, Dunn & Crutcher, what her clients used to do to her girls. This time the party on the receiving end paid—about $115,000 in lost legal fees.

$ $ $

William Lloyd Garrison
CIVIL WAR-ERA ABOLITIONIST

In 1829, Lloyd Garrison, then 24, started work as associate editor of the Baltimore, Maryland-based paper Genius of Universal Emancipation. Garrison used the paper to expound his views on "immediate and unconditional emancipation."

When Garrison discovered that a neighbor, Francis Todd, owned a slave ship, he was apoplectic. He described Todd and his partners in the Genius as "enemies of their own species," "highway robbers and murderers" who "should be sentenced to solitary con-finement for life." Mr. Todd sued for libel. The jury deliberated for less than 15 minutes before they found Garrison guilty.

The judge awarded Todd $50 plus another $50 for the cost of the action. On April 17, 1830, Garrison, unable to pay what at that time was a substantial amount, was locked up in a Baltimore debtors' prison. Garrison had completed seven weeks in jail when he received a letter from a New York silk trader, Arthur Tappan, offering to pay the $100 judgment and finance the republication of the Genius.

Garrison walked out of jail on June 5, 1830, after 49 days of incarceration.

$$\$\ \$\ \$$$

Paul Grueninger
WORLD WAR II HERO, SWISS POLICE CHIEF

Paul Grueninger, a Swiss police chief during World War II, faked Swiss passports for Jews fleeing Nazi Austria for Switzerland. He was working in the sleepy town of St. Gallen when the Swiss cowardly closed their borders to leave Jews at the mercy of the Nazi SS. Grueninger risked everything by secretly and illegally backdating Jewish passports. He saved 30,000 lives.

When the Swiss government discovered the scheme, it convicted Grueninger of fraud and fined and fired him. He died a penniless vagabond in 1972. In 1995, the Swiss, reacting to international outrage, revoked Grueninger's fraud sentence in the exact same courthouse where they had convicted him 55 years before.

$ $ $

Meriwether Lewis

MAPPED LOUISIANA TERRITORY

After Thomas Jefferson made the Louisiana Purchase in 1803, he sent Meriwether Lewis and William Clark to explore the new land. Lewis got paid by becoming governor of the Upper Louisiana Territory.

After Jefferson left office, his political enemies turned their backs on Lewis and cut off all financing. Stuck with the huge bills he ran up during explorations, and having no means to pay them, Lewis faced being thrown into a dank debtors' prison and possibly never getting out. He was on his way to Washington from St. Louis to re-plead his case when he apparently stabbed himself to death.

While some historians believe he was murdered, many believe Lewis killed himself rather than face prison.

$ $ $

Abraham Lincoln

16TH U.S. PRESIDENT

Abraham Lincoln, tired of splitting rails, and then living in New Salem, Illinois, opened a convenience store with his friend William F. Berry. He went into hock to buy the store and then borrowed some more to buy out a neighboring competitor. The problem was that nobody had any cash in the area to buy anything and the trading that did go on was barter. The Berry & Lincoln quickly "winked out," as the future president put it.

In need of a job, Lincoln campaigned for the state Legislature. While he won the election, he didn't get any votes from creditors. They were too busy suing him for nonpayment on the store's debts.

After celebrating, Lincoln noticed that his horse was missing. The sheriff had taken the horse, the saddle, the bridle and everything else Lincoln owned (which was not much) and put it up for auction.

Even that didn't pay the debts, which Lincoln referred to half-jokingly as the "National Debt." It would take Lincoln 17 years to repay the debt and regain solvency. (There was no bankruptcy law at that time.)

He once said to a friend: "That debt was the greatest obstacle I have ever met in my life; I had no way of speculating, and could not earn money except by labor, and to earn by labor eleven hundred dollars besides my living seemed the work of a lifetime. There was, however, but one way. I went to my creditors, and told them that if they would let me alone I would give them all I could earn over my living, as fast as I could earn it."

According to his law partner, William Herndon, Lincoln was still sending money back to New Salem creditors 20 years later as a member of Congress.

"It just sort of winked out."

—*ABRAHAM LINCOLN ON THE BANKRUPTCY OF HIS GROCERY STORE*

$ $ $

Cotton Mather
PURITAN LEADER

Some historians blame Cotton Mather's dire seventeenth-century sermons for the Salem witch-hunt. Mather paid for his sins by becoming the subject of something almost as painful—a creditor hunt.

Soon after warning his parishioners not to guarantee their neighbors' debts, Mather blindly agreed to guarantee the debts of his stepson-in-law, Nathan Howell.

Howell died immediately, owing more money than anyone imagined. Mather, as guarantor, suffered the hellfire wrath of creditors unpaid.

The minister was served multiple lawsuits at his home. After defaulting on several judgments, a humbled, desperate Mather turned to his congregation for help. The preacher's flock passed the plate to keep him out of debtors' prison.

But the lawsuits continued. Mather died without a penny in 1728. But death proved no debtor's sanctuary. Even as Mather faced the pearly gates, his creditors were still hounding him on earth. They claimed that Mather, when alive, fraudulently hid his personal library by giving it to his nephew, Samuel Sewall. The alleged fraud was never proven. The library has stayed with Sewall and his descendants to this day.

$ $ $

Eliot Ness

1920s FBI HERO

Eliot Ness was the government agent who, as the leader of the "Untouchables," put Al Capone away on tax-fraud charges. Ness began his crime-fighting career as a special agent for the U.S. Department of Justice in charge of the Prohibition Bureau in Chicago. After recruiting un-bribable agents (nicknamed by a newspaper columnist the "Untouchables") he raided Capone's gambling dens.

When he put Capone behind bars, Ness was 26 years old and a national hero. Like many who have achieved early meteoric success, Ness's life went downhill. After his wife left him in 1938, the lawman developed a reputation for drinking and womanizing. He started two businesses that failed. He left the government to join an alarm manufacturer but was fired for alcoholism.

Ness tried for a comeback by running for mayor of Cleveland against a Democratic incumbent, Tom Burke. He lost by a landslide. The campaign left him owing in the six-figures.

Trying to pay debts, Ness tried to cash in on his youthful glory by coauthoring a memoir called *The Untouchables*. The book bombed. A bankrupt Ness died of a heart attack in Coudersport, Pennsylvania, on May 16, 1957.

Less than a decade later, Hollywood turned his exploits into two hugely successful TV series, several made-for-TV specials and a blockbuster movie starring Kevin Costner.

$ $ $

Ronald Pelton

U.S. COUNTER-SPY AND TRAITOR

Ronald Pelton, a former computer analyst with the National Security Agency from 1964 to 1979, became infamous for selling the Russians secrets about the CIA's ability to monitor and decode foreign communications.

Intelligence agencies routinely fire personnel with extreme financial problems because of their vulnerability to foreign agents. That policy backfired with Pelton. Reduced to bankruptcy, the analyst betrayed his country for a mere $35,000 to pay living expenses.

Ronald Pelton was indicted on December 20, 1985, on six counts related to espionage. He was later convicted on one count of conspiracy and two counts of espionage and sentenced to three concurrent life sentences.

$ $ $

William Penn

FOUNDER OF PENNSYLVANIA

William Penn grew up as a rich kid, the son of a British admiral. At Oxford he rebelled by becoming Quaker, a very unpopular religion. In 1690, King Charles II granted Penn an estate in the American colonies, possibly to get him out of England. He turned it into a refuge for Quakers.

Penn turned operating control over to a treacherous underling. After Penn returned to England, the crooked caretaker borrowed to the hilt against the estate and disappeared with the money. Unable to pay creditors, Penn spent the rest of his days in a dark and filthy British debtors' prison. William Penn's Quaker refuge became the fifth American state in 1773.

$ $ $

Jean Baptiste Point du Sable
FOUNDER OF CHICAGO

Jean Baptiste Point du Sable, an African American from Sainte-Domingue (Haiti), lived among the Illinois Indians in St. Louis. He traveled the country with his Indian wife, trapping animals and trading their furs.

In 1779, he settled in an area near Lake Michigan known to the Indians as Chikagou. He built a house there—the first permanent settlement in the city now known as Chicago.

But, to the everlasting shame of the white man, as a black man he was cold-shouldered by later white settlers and died broke in 1818.

$ $ $

Charles Ponzi
NAMESAKE OF "PONZI SCHEME"

In 1920, Charles Ponzi, a Boston vegetable-stand man, started promising customers $125 in a week if they invested $100 today. He raised so much money that he gave up the stand. Of course, Ponzi repaid the old "investors" with the "investments" from new suckers. He did so well with this scam that it was named after him. After he ran out of new investors, the whole business, and eight banks, went up in smoke. 40,000 people lost about 70¢ on the dollar. Ponzi was jailed by the FBI for mail fraud on August 12, 1920.

He filed for personal bankruptcy, was deported and settled in Brazil, where he taught English as a foreign language until he died in a charity ward in 1949.

$ $ $

Oskar Schindler
SAVIOR OF 1,200 JEWS DURING WORLD WAR II

Known by everyone in his hometown as a "Gauner"—a swindler—Oskar Schindler came to Poland to see what bargains he could pick up after the Nazis took over.

He bribed the Germans into giving him a former enamelware factory (whose real owner was not in a position to complain).

Beginning production in 1939, he employed cheap Jewish workers from the nearby German-created Krakow ghetto.

An almost-free factory and almost-free labor—a capitalist heaven! Yet somehow, witnessing the bloodcurdling violence turned Schindler's head around. At the risk of immediate death, he protected Jewish workers by faking factory records. He would list the elderly as young workers. Doctors and lawyers were described as metalworkers. In the evening, Schindler would entertain SS and Wehrmacht officers, making friends and creating trust.

By feigning war production and smuggling medicine into Auschwitz, Schindler saved hundreds of lives. In 1944, he saved a thousand Jews by winning German approval for a new (phony) factory in Czechoslovakia.

His "children" eventually numbered 1,098—801 men and 297 women. Schindler spent all the money he had left on medicine, food and clothing for the Jews.

After the war, Schindler failed at ranching and cement manufacturing. He was on the way to debtors' prison when the people he saved and their children got him enough cash to pay off his debts and live comfortably. He died in 1974 and was buried on Mount Zion in Jerusalem.

$ $ $

Wilhelm Steinitz

AUSTRIAN CHESS MASTER

Born in Prague, Bohemia, (now the Czech Republic) in 1834,

Wilhelm Steinitz learned to play chess in the Viennese coffee houses as a way to hustle pocket money from tourists. By the age of 26 he was champion of Vienna and thoroughly obsessed with the game.

Eventually, Steinitz won the first official chess World Championship in New Orleans in 1886.

Although one of the greatest chess masters in history, Steinitz died bankrupt in a mental institution on August 12, 1900.

$$\$ \$ \$$$

Harry S. Truman
AMERICA'S 35TH PRESIDENT

After getting back home to Independence, Missouri, from the First World War, Truman opened a men's clothing store with his war buddy, Eddie Jacobson. The store did well at first by hawking fancy ties and cufflinks to returning doughboys who wanted off the farm ("after they'd seen Paree"). But after a while sales dried up.

Unwilling to face reality, Truman sunk more and more borrowed dollars into the empty store. He put up as collateral his 160-acre farm in Kansas. The store stayed empty and so did Truman's bank account.

In 1922, he finally threw in the towel and closed up shop. Truman was 38 years old , a business failure, broke and living with a mother-in-law who bossed him around the house. Just your typical future president of the United States.

Truman got out of debt the time-honored way—waiting for your creditor to die or go bankrupt. When the bank holding his

$8,944 debt went bankrupt in the 1930s, Truman bought the note for pennies on the dollar.

$ $ $

Preston Thomas Tucker

CREATOR OF THE 1940S WONDER CAR

After spending a career hawking cars for Ford and Chrysler, Preston Tucker formed the Tucker Corp. in 1946 to try to break into the high-volume car business. Tucker's "Car of the Future" broke new ground with standard pop-out safety windows, seatbelts and fully automatic transmission.

Before Tucker could turn out a single machine, the U.S. Securities Exchange Commission started poking around. While Tucker did end up producing 50 cars, a heavily publicized 1948 SEC fraud prosecution blackened the company's reputation. The fraud allegation was so baseless that Tucker won without putting one witness on the stand. The damage was done, however, and Tucker's company was liquidated for 18¢ on the dollar.

Tucker filed for personal bankruptcy. He died of lung cancer in 1956. Days before his death he got the financing to start another car company.

Historians have speculated that Tucker was the victim of not-so-subtle political sabotage, probably by other large automobile manufacturers who shall remain nameless to protect the author.

$$$

William M. Tweed
NEW YORK POLITICAL TYRANT

From 1865 to 1871 William Tweed ("Boss Tweed"), the corrupt political power broker, stole between $20 million and $200 million from New York City.

He was eventually convicted of 204 misdemeanor counts of approving fraudulent invoices. He died in a New York debtors' prison in 1878.

$$$

Amerigo Vespucci
AMERICA'S NAMESAKE

He was the first man to use the phrase "New World." Vespucci started out as a banker in Florence. Bored with banking, he became an explorer. Vespucci made his first discovery in 1499 while exploring for Spain. On January 1, 1502, he founded and named the harbor of Rio de Janeiro in honor of New Year's Day. He died penniless.

STATES WHERE YOU CAN STILL BE IMPRISONED FOR DEBT:

Rhode Island
Wisconsin

IN WISCONSIN YOU MAY BE JAILED IF A CREDITOR HAS A JUDGMENT AGAINST YOU FOR A TORT, SUCH AS NEGLIGENCE, AND YOU REFUSE TO PAY UP.

(Statutes Annotated Section 898.01)

IN BOTH STATES YOU CAN BE RELEASED IF YOU SWEAR YOU HAVE NO MONEY OR PROPERTY.

(GENERAL LAWS SECTION 10-13-1; WHITE V. TENTH DISTRICT COURT, 251 A.2D 539 (1969))

$ $ $

John Wayne

HOLLYWOOD FILM LEGEND

John Wayne thought he was wealthy. After all, he was a big movie star whose films had earned him millions. So when Saks Fifth Avenue called him to complain about a $3,200 unpaid bill, he dropped in on his money manager, Bo Roos, for an explanation. A cowering Roos admitted, after some excuses, that he had lost every cent.

Wayne rushed to his lawyer, Frank Belcher, who investigated and found no foul play, just bad judgment. A bewildered Wayne exclaimed, "I'll be god-damned. I was sure Bo had stolen it. Nobody's stupid enough to lose that much money!" Roos lost the Duke's money in bad real estate, Panama shrimp deals, Mexican hotels, dry oil wells and inflated expense accounts for Roos.

Wayne, of course, remained a big box office draw. In the 1970s, he was making over $1.5 million a year from acting. Yet even after going broke once, the star still fell for unusual and money-losing investments.

He invested in various unsuccessful schemes that included a treatment for baldness called "Hair Trigger Formula" and a plan to extract methane gas from cow manure. He also financed the development of "Product 76," a substance that supposedly could both cure skin ailments and insulate buildings.

Investment losses forced Wayne to do a wacky commercial for Bristol-Myers that had him dressed up in cowboy gear, hawking a headache pill. Only Wayne's huge earning power saved him from bankruptcy. He died in 1979 with an estate worth about $30 million—far less than it could have been.

$ $ $

Daniel Webster
AMERICAN SECRETARY OF STATE

When Webster was a boy he went to a county fair with his brother, Zeke. When his mother asked Daniel what happened to the quarter she had given him, Webster replied that he had spent it. She then asked Zeke the same question. Zeke replied, "I lent it to Daniel."

Throughout his life Webster continued to borrow money whenever and from whomever he could. He borrowed from his father-in-law, brothers-in-law, cousins and friends. He borrowed from political supporters and bankers. (Webster even pressured the painter of his official portrait for a $100 loan.) And he seldom paid anyone back. Webster's biggest loan was an 1836, $100,000 mortgage from the U.S.-run National Bank. A fly-by-night land hustler had assured Webster that his money would quintuple within a year. Two years later Webster sent a friend and neighbor, Hendy Thomas, to inspect his holdings. The land was either completely underwater or had dubious legal status. He defaulted on the loan.

So when Webster was tapped for U.S. Secretary of State in 1841, he had an embarrassing problem. He was joining the same government that was in the midst of foreclosing on his land. Webster had a private chat with Nicolas Biddle, the head of the bank, who had the bank forgive the loan.

Webster's compulsive borrowing (and failure to pay back his loans) often hurt his career. Congress raised the issue of Webster's debts to a few major capitalists as evidence of his incapacity to make impartial decisions. In 1851, Webster arranged to have a syndicate of Eastern bankers finance a $3 million indemnity to Mexico. The bankers that received this very profitable deal had also contributed to a political fund for Webster. Charles Allen, a Massachusetts Republican, openly charged Webster with taking bribes. The statesman's credibility never recovered.

Four days before his death he had his bankers, Corcoran & Riggs, cash a check that bounced. He died unable to pay household expenses.

Before he died, Webster played a key role in drafting a bill for the enactment of a federal uniform bankruptcy law. The Senate voted against the bill. But in 1898, a version of that bill finally passed. It created the federal bankruptcy laws that have existed in some form to the present day.

PATRIOTS

$ $ $

Samuel Adams

U.S. REVOLUTIONARY WAR AGITATOR; SIGNER OF THE DECLARATION OF INDEPENDENCE

Sam Adams, a cousin of President John Adams, started out as a banker and then became a brewer but couldn't make a go of either. He found his calling at age 40 as a rabble-rouser and organizer. In 1764, he won a seat to the Massachusetts Legislature. Eventually, he masterminded the Boston Tea Party.

As a reward, the Massachusetts Legislature voted to send him to the Constitutional Convention. Adams was so broke that another attendee, John Hancock, had to spot him the carriage fare.

$$$

Benedict Arnold

REVOLUTIONARY WAR TRAITOR

After Benedict Arnold's plot to turn West Point over to the British failed, the commander in chief of British forces in America, General Sir Henry Clinton, issued him a check for $6,000. That money proved to be his last serious income.

Arnold moved to New Brunswick, Canada, a loyalist refuge. He bought a lumberyard, a shipyard and local building lots. The former hero of the Battle of Saratoga lost his money in constant libel and commercial litigations. A former business partner accused Arnold of torching a building for the insurance. On top of that, his businesses foundered. The local citizens burned Arnold in effigy in front of his house—not exactly great PR. He found out that no one likes or trusts a traitor.

He fled to England in 1897 and ran up debts attempting to finance privateers. As if cursed, everything he tried failed. The former hero of the victorious Battle of Saratoga sickened and died with the knowledge that he was leaving his beautiful wife and young children unprotected and destitute.

"Gone to Kentucky."

—*WRITTEN ON THE BACK
OF A JUDGMENT AGAINST
DANIEL BOONE*

$$$

Daniel Boone
AMERICAN FRONTIERSMAN

Legendary in the 1760s as a hunter and trapper, Daniel Boone never made a great living. While he borrowed to finance his fur-hunting expeditions, he often came back empty-handed. Other times, he gave up horses, traps and guns to unfriendly Indians to save his life.

As a result, he was no hero to local bankers. His friend, the lawyer Richard Henderson, said of him that "he had the honor of having more suits entered against him for debt than any other man of his day." In fact, according to Henderson, Boone's motivation for exploring and settling wild Kentucky was to escape creditors back East. Eventually, a Virginia judge finally issued a judgment and a warrant for Boone's arrest on a debt. On the back of the judgment a clerk later scribbled "Gone to Kentucky."

$$$

Jacob DeHaven
REVOLUTIONARY WAR HERO

Jacob DeHaven reportedly lent $450,000 in gold and supplies, everything he had, to the Continental Congress in 1777 to feed troops at Valley Forge. The alleged loan was never repaid. DeHaven died penniless in 1812.

The DeHavens would like the money back. As recently as 1990, the DeHaven family descendants got together and sued the U.S. for $105.3 billion, inclusive of interest. The family says that it is willing to accept "reasonable payment."

$ $ $

William Duer
NEW YORK DELEGATE TO THE CONTINENTAL CONGRESS AND A SIGNER OF THE ARTICLES OF CONFEDERATION

English born, William Duer made a fortune as a New Yorker supplying masts to the British Royal Navy. During the American Revolution, Duer became one of the largest contractors supplying goods to the Continental Army. He invested the profits in huge land speculations. The panic of 1790 ruined him. His arrest for debt sparked the financial panic of 1792. He spent the rest of his life in debtors' prison.

$ $ $

Button Gwinnett
SIGNER OF THE DECLARATION OF INDEPENDENCE FROM GEORGIA

Burton Gwinnett represented the state of Georgia at the Continental Congress. Prior to his career in politics, he went bankrupt as a planter on St. Catherine's Island off the Georgia coast. As a known rebel, the British burned his last remaining property. He died at age

45 from wounds suffered during a duel with a political rival.

Gwinnett's signature is, because of its rarity, currently one of the world's most valuable and worth many times the politician's old debts.

$$$

John Hart
SIGNER OF DECLARATION OF INDEPENDENCE FROM NEW JERSEY

John Hart was the largest landowner in Hopewell Township, New Jersey, with over 600 acres. On November 13, 1776, British and Hessian troops invaded the state. The Hessians damaged his farm. Before the Battle of Monmouth, General Washington and 12,000 troops camped on his fields during the growing season. His property ruined, Hart died in 1779.

$$$

Thomas Jefferson
THIRD U.S. PRESIDENT

The third U.S. president and author of the Declaration of Independence died with creditors banging on his door. Jefferson went into debt at the White House paying for state dinners for diplomats, congressmen and senators. The government never reimbursed him. When he left office in 1808 he was in debt in the amount of $24,000 (around $500,000 in today's dollars.)

Back at Monticello, most of Jefferson's income came from sell-

"I must sell my
house and all here
and carry my family
to Bedford where
I have not even a
log hut to put my
head into."

—*THOMAS JEFFERSON AT AGE 82,
UPON BEING TURNED DOWN FOR
AN $80,000 INTEREST-FREE GOVERNMENT
LOAN. HE DIED SOON THEREAFTER.*

ing tobacco and flour crops. He also had a nail-manufacturing business on the side.

After 1815, droughts decimated his plantation. At the same time, the British (maybe in payback for the Declaration) flooded the market with cheap nails, wiping out Jefferson's nail operations.

Worst of all, Jefferson had agreed to guarantee a $21,200 loan for his son-in-law and former Virginia governor Wilson Cary. Cary was bankrupted by the depression of 1819, the country's first major depression.

Jefferson's liability on the note finally brought the wolf to the door. Creditors threatened to liquidate Monticello. Like many a modern credit-card victim, he borrowed from one bank to pay another until he burned out his credit.

Jefferson died in debt on July 4, 1826. Creditors foreclosed on Monticello three years later. Exactly 100 years later, in 1926, the federal government bought Monticello and turned it into a national museum.

$ $ $

Henry "Lighthorse Harry" Lee III
*REVOLUTIONARY WAR HERO; FRIEND OF WASHINGTON;
FATHER OF ROBERT E. LEE*

Richard Henry Lee or "Lighthorse Harry" Lee, as he was known to his troops, twice spent time in jail for debts after the Revolutionary War. Before that, Lee was a war hero, confidant of George Washington and governor of Virginia.

During the 1780s, Lee speculated in Western lands using borrowed funds. The expected deluge of European buyers never materialized. Land values collapsed and Lee began passing bad checks to creditors.

The war hero was locked up in a debtors' prison in Westmoreland County, Virginia. After he was released in 1810, upon a declaration of bankruptcy and the turnover of all his property, Lee was supported by his wife's inheritance.

Robert E. Lee used to talk of being a young boy and asking why strange men came into the house and took the furniture away. Maybe that's why Robert E. Lee never left the army and steady paychecks.

$$\$ \ \$ \ \$$$

Pierre-Charles L'Enfant
ARCHITECT WHO DESIGNED WASHINGTON, D.C.

Born in France, and educated as an engineer, Pierre-Charles L'Enfant joined Lafayette in America to fight the American Revolution in 1777. Still in the service after the war, he drafted plans for the new federal city.

Hot-tempered, L'Enfant fought with his boss, who fired him in 1792. In a moment of pique, he refused payment for his work planning the capital.

Later destitute, the architect unsuccessfully hounded Congress for compensation, often appearing drunk at meetings. He lived out his years bankrupt and supported by friends.

Buried in Bladensburg, Maryland, L'Enfant was later disinterred by an Act of Congress and reinterred in the National Cemetery at Arlington with full military honors. The service was attended by President William Howard Taft and attended by members of Congress.

$ $ $

Robert Morris

FINANCED AMERICAN REVOLUTION

In 1778, the American Revolution ground to a halt when Continental troops refused to march on Yorktown without one month's back pay. An eighteenth-century Michael Milkin, Robert Morris quickly raised the $40,000 needed to pay the troops.

A close friend of George Washington, Morris was one of the signers of the Declaration of Independence. He single-handedly financed Patriot soldiers by starting the first national bank.

After the war, Morris speculated in real estate. Having inside information that the capital would be built in Washington, D.C., he bet everything he had and then some to buy thousands of acres in the area. Real estate prices collapsed when foreign buyers suddenly sold out.

Well in the red, Morris sat in debtors' prison for three years. President George Washington would occasionally drop by to shoot the breeze. Morris died destitute at age 71.

$ $ $

Thomas Nelson, Jr.
PATRIOT, SIGNER OF DECLARATION OF INDEPENDENCE FROM VIRGINIA

A former governor of Virginia, Thomas Nelson commanded the Virginia militia during the siege of Yorktown during the Revolutionary War. When British General Cornwallis used his mansion, the Nelson House, for his headquarters, Nelson commanded that his own property be blown to bits.

After the war, Nelson sold off the rest of his belongings to pay his hungry troops.

$ $ $

Thomas Paine
REVOLUTIONARY WAR AGITATOR

Paine wrote Common Sense, which George Washington called the "spark" of the American Revolution.

Paine first went bankrupt as a British corset maker. After that, he got fired from his job as a government tax collector for demanding higher wages. His rambunctiousness caught the amused eye of Benjamin Franklin, who brought him back to the colonies. Paine's Common Sense was the first American blockbuster. Not only did it start the American Revolution, it brought some much needed cash to Thomas Paine.

$$$

Daniel Shays
LEADER OF SHAYS REBELLION

Daniel Shays was a veteran of Bunker Hill and former captain in the Revolutionary Army. After the war he farmed in Western Massachusetts. When the American Revolution ended in 1783, the country was in economic chaos. New England states taxed working stiffs to pay back the wealthy merchants who had helped finance the Revolution. Tax collectors with judgments seized furniture, grain, livestock and farms. Farmers were thrown into debtors' prisons.

Wondering why they had fought the war, the farmers dusted off their muskets. Shays, leading the farmers, stopped the lawsuits by simply burning down every courthouse he could find. A few months later federal troops reestablished order. The U.S. sentenced Shays to be hanged, but later pardoned him because of his service during the Revolution.

Jefferson was speaking about Shays' Rebellion when he said, "a little rebellion now and then is a good thing."

$ $ $

James Wilson

First U.S. Supreme Court Justice

James Wilson was one of only six men who signed both the Declaration of Independence and the U.S. Constitution. He drafted important parts of the United States Constitution and during the 1787 Constitutional Convention his influence was second only to James Madison. Wilson served nine years as one of the country's first Supreme Court Justices.

Not happy on a judge's salary, Wilson made a highly leveraged investment in four million acres of New York and Pennsylvania undeveloped real estate. After land values crashed, the judge was hopelessly in debt. Debtors' prison loomed. With the sheriff in pursuit, the former highest judge in the land fled by carriage to Burlington, New Jersey. He died while hiding at the home of James Iredell, a fellow Supreme Court Justice.

FIVE PRESIDENTS DIED WITH DEBTS THEY COULDN'T PAY:

Jefferson owed
$107,273.63

Monroe owed
$70,000

William Henry Harrison
owed an unknown amount

Tyler owed
$2,000

Grant owed
$150,000

POLITICIANS

$ $ $

Jeffrey Archer
MEMBER OF PARLIAMENT, GREAT BRITAIN

Oxford-educated Jeffrey Archer was elected to the House of Commons in 1969 at the age of 29. He resigned under pressure five years later amidst a financial scandal that apparently ended in his bankruptcy. Needing money quickly, Archer sat down at his kitchen table and wrote a best-selling novel, *Not a Penny More, Not a Penny Less*.

In 1985, he became Margaret Thatcher's Tory Party chairman. The following year he was forced to resign due to a scandal involving allegations that he paid £2,000 in hush money to a prostitute. He sued the newspaper, the Daily Star for libel and in 1987 won $820,000, Britain's largest settlement ever.

$ $ $

Tommy Brooks
MISSISSIPPI STATE SENATOR

Tommy Brooks served in the Mississippi Legislature for 29 years until a grand jury indicted him on extortion charges in March 1985. Earlier that month Brooks, then 60, allegedly accepted a brown paper bag stuffed with $15,000 from an undercover agent. FBI agents in the state's capital later arrested him. Brooks had filed for personal bankruptcy shortly before the incident.

$ $ $

Ky Nguyen Cao
PRIME MINISTER OF SOUTH VIETNAM

Ky served as Premier of Vietnam from 1965 to 1967 during the Vietnam War. After the Communist takeover in 1975, he settled in Southern California and opened the Saigon Deli in Westminster, California.

The 54-year-old former world figure filed for bankruptcy in November 1983. His debts included a $20,000 gambling debt to Caesars Palace in Las Vegas, and $615,000 owed to banks throughout the country. His bankruptcy papers listed almost $700,000 in assets—mostly consisting of his $250,000 home and a $400,000 liquor store. Ky, who has experienced more twists and turns

"We are enjoying life. [The bankruptcy] is just another difficult step that we will take during our lifetime. You try to do the right thing, but sometimes it's just your destiny."

—KY NGUYEN CAO ON HIS BANKRUPTCY

than most men, said at the time that he was enjoying life despite his financial problems.

$$$

Dennis Carpenter
CALIFORNIA STATE SENATOR

A personal advisor to President Ronald Reagan, Dennis Carpenter filed for bankruptcy on June 2, 1983.

$$$

John Connally
THREE-TERM TEXAS GOVERNOR;
FORMER TREASURY SECRETARY

The son of a poor farmer, Connally became a three-time governor of Texas and U.S. Treasury Secretary.

Connally entered the real estate business with his partner Ben Barnes, shortly before the collapse of the market in Texas. The partnership had borrowed heavily to develop $200 million worth of properties in Austin, on South Padre Island on the Texas Gulf Coast, and in Houston. Unbelievably, Connally put himself personally on the line for many of his real estate deals. Ruined by the collapse of oil, gas and real estate values in the late 1980s, Connally filed for Chapter 11 bankruptcy in August of 1987. The former Treasury Secretary had debts totaling $93 million but assets of only $13 million.

"Things didn't work out exactly as we planned."

—*JOHN CONNALLY*

Worth at his peak over $100 million, Connally was reduced to auctioning off his living room furniture and highly personal mementos on his front lawn. Just a few months before, his home had graced the glossy pages of Architectural Digest. Now its contents were emptied while strangers lined up to bargain hunt.

Connally never displayed bitterness or meanness during an experience that must have been pure torture. He and his wife even served tea during the auction. The former politician won national admiration for his dignity under pressure. Connally died in June of 1993 at age 76.

$$ $ $

Benjamin Disraeli
BRITISH PRIME MINISTER

In 1824, a teenage Disraeli somehow borrowed large sums to speculate on South American mining stocks. When the shares plummeted, Disraeli was left with a debt of £7,000—around a $250,000 in today's U.S. dollars.

Hopelessly in debt, perhaps Disraeli figured that more debt wouldn't make a difference. Anyway, Disraeli upped his borrowing. After his stock market debacle, he hit his uncle George Basevi up for ?1000, which he never repaid. He took hundreds of pounds from his friend Benjamin Austin. The future prime minister borrowed to the hilt to pay for his first political campaign in 1832.

Under British law, members of Parliament can't be arrested for debt. Disraeli admitted openly that he stayed in office because if he got out he'd be jailed.

By 1842, Disraeli owed over £24,000. Without telling his new wife, Mary Anne, he bought time by mortgaging the entire contents of their house. Eventually his debts grew to £60,000. (This was a time when a family could live comfortably for a year on £100.)

Disraeli's money problems eventually went away with an inheritance from an admiring widow, Sarah Brydges Willyams, and low-interest loans from political supporters.

$$ $ \$ \$ \$ $$

Ulysses S. Grant

LED UNION ARMY IN CIVIL WAR, U.S. PRESIDENT

When Grant left the presidency in 1880, he relocated to a Manhattan townhouse on tony East 66th Street. Never a rich man, Grant looked forward to a life of wealth and ease. His son pitched him a partnership with Ferdinand Ward, a young Wall Street hotshot whom the tabloids called "the young Napoleon of Finance." Impressed, Grant sold his farm in Galena, Ohio, and invested all the proceeds, $100,000, to start Grant & Ward. The famous hero's name attracted big money investors from senators and tycoons all over the country.

But Ward was running a pre-Ponzi Ponzi scheme. Within a few months investors were receiving returns of up to 40 percent from money that flowed in from new "investors." When the scam ran out of victims, Ward pressured Grant to get more money. Told that the firm only needed a short-term loan, Grant borrowed $150,000 from

Ulysses S. Grant:

Forced to write his memoirs so his family could eat.

a wealthy admirer, William H. Vanderbilt.

The firm's debts were by that time insurmountably huge. Grant & Ward shut its doors, leaving investors owed $16 million. Ward was sent to Sing Sing.

Grant was humiliated and exonerated but broke. The shock came so quickly that the Grant household was down to $180 in cash. An anonymous admirer donated $1,000 to pay for groceries.

That summer Grant learned that he had cancer in the throat and had less than a year to live. To bring in money, Grant accepted an offer to write articles for *Century* magazine at $500 per article. Mark Twain, who had met Grant previously, offered to publish his memoirs. Twain had self-published *The Adventures of Huckleberry Finn* that same year with enormous success.

The general quietly transferred the income rights from the unpublished manuscript to his wife, Julia, to save it from rapacious creditors.

Grant finally finished his memoirs on July 19, 1885, and died less than a week later. More than 150,000 copies had already been ordered, guaranteeing the book's success. His book grossed over $450,000 for his family. It is still in print.

$$ $ $ $ $$

Ed Herschler
WYOMING GOVERNOR

A Democrat in the fiercely Republican state of Wyoming, Ed Herschler governed for three terms as the most popular politician in the state. In September 1985, his 18,500-acre Yellowstone Ranch failed. Herschler filed for bankruptcy to discharge personal guarantees on the ranch. He listed $5.9 million in debts.

$ $ $

George McGovern
U.S. SENATOR, FORMER PRESIDENTIAL CONTENDER

Some people say that the quickest way to turn a liberal Democrat into a conservative Republican is to have him open a business. That theory was tested when George McGovern, the former 1972 Democratic presidential candidate, opened in inn in Stratford, Connecticut.

He filed for bankruptcy on January 20, 1991, after the inn went out of business. McGovern and his partners owed back state taxes on the three-story, 150-room inn, which had filed for Chapter 11 bankruptcy earlier that year. The former senator had bought the inn in 1988.

McGovern put the chief blame on the recession that hit New England at that time. But he also admitted that some wounds were self-inflicted—the taxes and government regulations he had supported helped put the business underwater.

"[To] run a place the way it should be run."

—GEORGE MCGOVERN EXPLAINING
WHY HE WAS DROPPING OUT OF
POLITICS TO OPEN AN INN

$ $ $

Edward Mezvinsky
U.S. CONGRESSMAN

A Democratic congressman from Iowa during the 1970s, Edward Mezvinsky served on the House Judiciary Committee that voted to impeach President Richard Nixon. A former Maryland state senator, Mezvinsky filed in Philadelphia, Pennsylvania to discharge a $1.1 million loan from Jefferson Bank, $14,000 in utility bills owed to PECO Energy Co. and a disputed fraud allegation claiming $1.15 million.

$ $ $

C. Edward Middlebrooks, Jr.
MARYLAND STATE SENATOR

A Republican state senator from Anne Arundel Country, C. Edward Middlebrooks filed Chapter 7 due to sour real estate investments.

$ $ $

Robert Price
FORMER U.S. CONGRESSMAN

A Republican from Texas, Robert Price filed a Chapter 11 bankruptcy to avert the sale of his 9,600-acre ranch by the Small Business and

Farm Administration. Price owed $2.3 million to the SBFA. The filing halted Price's candidacy during the 1983 congressional election campaign.

$ $ $

Fife Symington
ARIZONA GOVERNOR

When you run for governor on the basis of your business acumen and file for bankruptcy after you are elected, you are bound to raise some eyebrows. Such was the situation when the personal finances of Arizona Governor Fife Symington began to unravel in office.

Before Symington filed for bankruptcy, he offered to pay creditors 25 percent from his state paycheck. Creditors balked and Symington filed, listing debts of $25 million and assets of $61,000.

The governor's financial woes began long before his election. They stem from several failed real estate projects for which Symington personally guaranteed the financing. One, the Mercado Mall in Phoenix, failed to meet its expenses from day one. Symington personally guaranteed a $10 million loan from six pension funds. These pension funds sued for repayment, causing Symington to resort to bankruptcy.

Later, Symington was convicted of fraud and extortion for improperly arranged financing for his projects with the funds of a bank on which he served as director. Symington was pardoned by President Clinton in 2001.

$ $ $

Craig Washington
U.S. CONGRESSMAN

Craig Washington served as a respected member of the Texas House of Representatives from 1973 to 1982. He was elected in the 18th District of Texas after U.S. Representative Mickey Leland died in a 1989 airplane crash. Reportedly, the drop in income from his work as a private attorney to a congressional salary contributed to his financial problems. His personal bankruptcy filing listed $205,000 in federal taxes. Washington lost his seat to Sheila Jackson Lee in 1994.

$ $ $

Glenn Way
UTAH STATE SENATOR

Glenn Way, a fiscally conservative Republican from Spanish Fork, Utah, filed for bankruptcy in July 1998. The Senator listed $65,000 in unsecured debts and $122,000 in secured debt. Way's debts grew out of control due to a failed investment in a Provo pizza parlor in 1995 and medical problems suffered by his fourth child.

CELEBRITIES

$$$

John Wayne Bobbitt
CASTRATION CELEBRITY AND PORN STAR

Bobbitt gained worldwide fame when his wife, Lorena Bobbitt, sliced off the Manassa, Virginia, resident's penis with a razor in the early morning of June 23, 1993. Part of the fame grew out of the celebrated operation wherein urologist Jim Sehn, then 48, and plastic surgeon David Berman, then 36, successfully reattached the severed organ.

Lorena Bobbitt had, in a panic, thrown the penis out of a car window onto the roadside near a 7-Eleven. The police found the penis using searchlights and delivered it to Dr. Sehn in a Ziploc bag, inside a brown paper lunch sack. The penis was quickly put into a bowl of ice. The 12-hour surgery succeeded. Bobbitt was able to achieve erection. To prove that to unbelievers, he later starred in his

"He stiffed us."

—THE DOCTORS WHO REATTACHED JOHN BOBBITT'S PENIS (BOBBITT'S BANKRUPTCY WIPED OUT THE MEDICAL BILLS FROM THE OPERATION.)

very own porno movie. The Bobbitt case brought instant renown to Sehn and Berman, but they never got paid. Bobbitt had no health insurance and filed for bankruptcy soon after the surgery.

$$$

Lammot (Motsey) du Pont Copeland, Jr.
HEIR TO THE DU PONT FORTUNE

Lammot du Pont was the first du Pont to file for bankruptcy. He had assets of $25.7 million and liabilities of over $59 million.

$$$

Morton Downey, Jr.
TV TALK SHOW STAR

Just seven months after Downey's nationally syndicated talk show ended, the talk show host filed for Chapter 11 relief in Newark, New Jersey. He claimed $100 in assets and debts of over $2.3 million, including a $600,000 mortgage and $500,000 in federal taxes. It was the fourth time Downey has filed for bankruptcy. He previously filed for bankruptcy in Ohio in 1985.

$$$

Jean Ronald Getty
ONE OF J. PAUL GETTY'S FIVE SONS

The billionaire oilman cut Ronald out of the family trust, possibly due to resentments towards Ronald's mother, Adolphine. Ronald Getty filed for bankruptcy in 1982. He now lives in Germany and is reportedly supported by his brothers.

$$$

Bernard Goetz
SUBWAY VIGILANTE

On December 22, 1984, Bernard Goetz shot four young black men in a Manhattan subway car. Goetz, a 34-year-old freelance electrician, said the men had threatened him with a screwdriver and tried to rob him.

A New York jury acquitted him of attempted murder and assault but convicted him of criminal possession of an unlicensed weapon. He spent 250 days in jail.

Darrel Cabey, one of the alleged muggers, claimed that the four men were merely panhandling when Goetz started shooting. Cabey, whom Goetz paralyzed with a shot to the back, sued the vigilante and won $43 million.

Goetz ,who thought the shooting "could be looked on" as a public service, filed for bankruptcy on April 29, 1996. He listed as creditors Cabey; his mother, Shirley; and his criminal defense lawyers Barry Slotnick, Mark Baker, and Joseph and Robert Kelner.

Goetz currently lives abroad.

$ $ $

Margaux Hemingway

HEMINGWAY DAUGHTER, ACTRESS, MODEL

The oldest daughter of Ernest Hemingway, Margaux Hemingway burst on the modeling scene with a Time magazine cover photo in 1975. Her gorgeous looks and family pedigree got her a ticket to the Beautiful People party scene.

Eventually, in the 1980s, Hemingway succumbed to serious bouts with alcoholism and bulimia. She filed for bankruptcy shortly after shooting explicit nude scenes for *Playboy* magazine in 1990. She listed $815,000 in debt and negligible assets. Like her father, grandfather, uncle and aunt, Hemingway apparently committed suicide. She was found dead in her one-room Santa Monica, California, apartment of an alleged drug overdose.

$ $ $

E. Howard Hunt

WATERGATE PLUMBER

Life surely has been adventurous for E. Howard Hunt, a man who ran covert operations for the CIA, snooped for the office of the president of the United States and later became a leading figure in the downfall of that president.

It was that final adventure that proved costly. Hunt was one of the five burglars caught inside Democratic National Headquarters at the Watergate Hotel. Since he had to pay for his own legal counsel, the legal bills far outlasted the scandal.

Hunt filed for personal bankruptcy in June 1995, listing debts of $234,000 and assets of $147,182. His assets included a 1989 Mercury that Hunt claimed needed repairs. Hunt's publisher, St. Martin's, was listed as one of the creditors.

$ $ $

Barbara Hutton
Heiress

Granddaughter of F.W. Woolworth and daughter of Franklin Hutton, cofounder of E.F. Hutton, Barbara Hutton inherited $50 million in 1933, making her one of the richest women in the world. The poor little rich girl went through seven husbands, mostly titled European scoundrels, who separated her from her money.

Hutton had just $3,500 in her checking account when she died.

$ $ $

Larry King

TV TALK SHOW STAR

Some strike it rich and then blow it. Others hit bottom and then score beyond anybody's wildest dreams. Such is the case with Larry King, the star host of the Larry King Show. King filed for bankruptcy protection when he was still a fledgling radio show host in 1971.

King was born Lawrence Harvey Zeiger in 1933 to the owner of a bar and grill and his seamstress wife. He got into the radio business in Miami. By 1970, King had started doing celebrity interviews and became a local hit.

King's need to be a big shot led him to date Playboy Bunnies, tool around in Cadillacs, bet heavily on the ponies and generally live way beyond his means. He got away with it for a while by smooth talking his bankers and bookies.

In 1971, a friend named Lou Wolfson ran into trouble with the Securities and Exchange Commission. King suggested retaining the future U.S. Attorney General John Mitchell, with whom he had a contact. After Mitchell turned the case down, King kept the money paid to him by Wolfson that he was supposed to give to Mitchell. On December 20, 1971, the Miami police arrested King on grand larceny charges. The charges were later dropped when the statute of limitations ran out.

Fired from his job, separated from his wife, King started drifting. He hit the highways, surviving hand to mouth doing freelance radio work. He was 38 years old.

Finally King got the Magic Call. Ed Little, an old boss now at the Mutual Radio Network in Washington, needed King to host a talk show. Starting with just 23 stations, King's network eventually ballooned to over 323, becoming one of radio's most spectacular success stories.

But in 1978 King was still making $26,000 and owed $352,000, including $14,000 in gambling debts. Sharon, his new wife, had him declare bankruptcy the same year he started his new job. The debts included $55 owed to a Miami florist shop, $14,000 owed to Hialeah Race Track and $90,387 owed to a private lender in Florida.

Today King could pay those debts out of petty cash.

$ $ $

James W. Marshall
SPARKED 1890'S GOLD RUSH

A New Jersey native, James Marshall took up his father's carpenter trade before lighting out for California. Marshall ended up setting up with local landowner John Sutton to run a sawmill in Cullomah Valley.

While examining the turbine of the American River-powered mill, something unusual happened.

After shutting off the water from the race I stepped into it, near the lower end, and there, upon the rock, about six inches beneath the surface of the water, I discovered the gold. I was entirely alone at the time....I then collected four or five pieces and went up to Mr.

Scott (who was working on the carpenters bench making the mill wheel) with the pieces in my hand and said, 'I have found it.' 'What is it?' inquired Scott. 'Gold,' I answered.

Hordes of scraggly miners swept down almost overnight on the quiet mill site and dug up every inch of the land. Marshall, whose find made countless others millionaires, failed to get the legal rights to his gold fields. His sawmill went bankrupt since all the workers quit to pan for gold. Crazed gangs beat him up so he'd lead them to gold.

He sold his ranch on Butte Creek to invest in a mine near Kelsey. It flopped. Eventually, Marshall became an alcoholic. He drifted around California drunk most of the time until he died of exposure in 1885.

$ $ $

Jackie Mason
JEWISH COMEDIAN

A rabbi from a long line of rabbis, Mason found his second calling when so many people laughed during his sermons the he "began charging a cover and a minimum." After his big break on the Ed Sullivan Show, Mason's career nose-dived.

He went bankrupt in 1983 after investing all his money in plays and movies that failed. In 1987, the comedian made a stunning comeback with the hit Broadway show *The World According to Me!* telling the same jokes "I told for 20 years."

"The last few years of my life have been a little like a long ride in a Poop de Ville with the bottom down."

—*PAT PAULSON ON HIS BANKRUPTCY*

$ $ $

Donald Nixon
RICHARD NIXON'S BROTHER

Former President Richard Nixon's younger brother filed for bankruptcy in 1961, owing his creditors about $200,000. Donald Nixon incurred debts in connection with an investment in Nixon's, Inc., a chain of Southern California restaurants. Billionaire Howard Hughes lent the younger Nixon $206,000 in a failed attempt to help him ward off disaster. The Hughes loan, once made public, helped Nixon lose to Kennedy in the 1960 presidential race.

$ $ $

Pat Paulson
AMERICAN COMEDIAN

Pat Paulson's work on the Smothers Brothers Comedy Hour earned him national recognition and an Emmy award in 1968. Paulson ran into trouble in the 1980s when the IRS claimed $270,000 in back taxes and his Asti, California, winery business ran up $1.5 million in debts. Paulson filed for bankruptcy to thwart an IRS sale of his winery.

Asked about his bankruptcy, Paulson recounted "I once told Tommy Smothers, 'If I could just get the money and women straightened out, the rest of my life would be easy.' Tommy looked at me, puzzled, for a moment, and then asked, 'The rest of your life? After money and women, what else is there?'"

$$$

Susan Powter
FITNESS GURU

The bleach-blonde trainer made millions for her company with her Stop the Insanity! workout videos in the 1990s. She filed for Chapter 11 in 1995 while lawsuits flew between Powter and her partners.

Powter's revenue was allegedly controlled by her estranged partners, Gerald and Richard Frankel, 50 percent owners of the Susan Powter Corp. Powter earned a salary based on profits but, she says, had no control over revenue. Powter called the arrangement "slave labor." The trainer listed $3.3 million in debts and only $500,000 to $999,000 in assets.

$$$

Anna Nicole Smith
AMERICAN SUPERMODEL

A Texas native, Anna Nicole Smith became one of the world's best-known models through GUESS Clothing ads beginning in 1992. GUESS founder, Paul Marciano, hired her after he saw her in Playboy magazine. Texas oilman J. Howard Marshall, 90 years young, and worth about $900 million, saw the same issue and decided he needed Anna to while away his golden years. The pair married, Marshall soon died, and full-scale legal war exploded over Marshall's estate. The legal costs and other lawsuits forced Smith to filed for bankruptcy.

The blonde sex goddess later stunned the nation by winning her lawsuit and walking away with $550 million. *Playboy* celebrated the event with an explicit pictorial feature.

$ $ $

Wolfman Jack, a.k.a. Robert Smith
RADIO JOCK STAR

Brooklyn-born Robert Smith, also known as Wolfman Jack, exposed American teenagers to rock 'n' roll from an illegal Mexican radio station. By the 1970s though, disco was king and the Wolfman was broke.

His role in *American Graffiti,* a blockbuster movie directed by George Lucas, was what kept the wolf from the Wolfman's door. Lucas paid Smith only $3,000 for his role but when movie sales went ballistic, he voluntarily gave Smith a generous percentage of the revenues.

$$$

Gloria Vanderbilt
MOTHER OF CLOTHES DESIGNER GLORIA VANDERBILT

Gloria Vanderbilt filed for bankruptcy in 1938. She was the first Vanderbilt ever to file for bankruptcy. Huge legal bills over guardianship of her daughter put her in the red. Vanderbilt also lost money in her own clothing-design business investment. Her daughter eventually made good in the same business by grossing over $160 million in designer jeans.

MUSICIANS

$$$

Toni Braxton
AMERICAN R&B SUPERSTAR

This 1990s recording artist sold more than $179 million in records but was only paid 35¢ per $17 album. Braxton also lost millions in bad investments. The five-time Granny Award-winner filed for bankruptcy in January 1998 as a result of disputes over her contracts with Arista and LaFace records.

Braxton continues to be enormously popular. In October 2000, her albums *Secrets* and *The Heat* were both declared platinum records many times over.

$ $ $

Anita Bryant
AMERICAN ANTI-GAY ACTIVIST

Once a runner up in the Miss America beauty pageant and later a TV spokesperson of the Florida Citrus Commission, Anita Bryant galvanized gays when she started an anti-homosexual group called Save Our Children. Bryant was fired by the orange growers when gays fought back by boycotting orange juice. She and her husband filed for bankruptcy in 1997 to reorganize debts of up to $10 million.

$ $ $

Luther Campbell
RAP STAR

Luther Campbell gained national notoriety in 1991 defending his art against Florida obscenity charges. Campbell eventually beat obscenity charges in Hollywood, Florida, for performing rap lyrics from his album *As Nasty As They Wanna Be*. The national publicity helped sell more than a million copies.

But in 1995, MC Shy D, a rapper signed to Campbell's record company, Luke Records, won a $1.6 million lawsuit for royalty infringement. Campbell also faced a lawsuit from his former lawyer, Joe Weinberger.

Campbell, who had to give up a private 36-hole golf course and yacht, filed bankruptcy to wipe out the debts.

$$$

George Clinton
KING OF FUNK MUSIC

The creator of "Funkadelic," George "Dr. Funkstein" Clinton went broke when he found himself on the receiving end of a breach-of-contract lawsuit. Restrained from recording, Clinton filed for personal bankruptcy in 1985.

After overcoming a crack addiction, he bounced back with the group "The P-Funk All Stars" and then started a solo career with the aptly named album, *Hey Man...Smell My Finger*.

$$$

David Crosby
ROCK SUPERSTAR

David Crosby was a founding member of the Byrds and is currently a member of *Crosby, Stills and Nash*. A cocaine addiction bankrupted Crosby and landed him in jail.

In 1985, Crosby spent a year behind bars for violating a plea bargain. When he was released in August 1986, he moved in with his future biographer, Carl Gottlieb, in West Hollywood, Los Angeles. Gottlieb gave the singer a free home and spending money. When Crosby left jail he owed the IRS over $1 million in back taxes. He filed for bankruptcy relief later that year. In 1987 and 1988,

Crosby, Stills and Nash toured the U.S. and Crosby began repaying debts.

$ $ $

Vic Damone
AMERICAN SINGER

Brooklyn-born Vic Damone got his start as an usher at New York's Paramount Theater. A popular crooner and actor in the 1940s and '50s, Damone lost his audience in the '60s.

In 1963 he co-signed a loan for $250,000 with two business partners. His partners fled to Beirut, Lebanon, with the loan proceeds, leaving Damone with the personal liability. When the singer told his loyal wife, Judy Rawlins, the bad news she sued him for divorce. Damone filed for bankruptcy.

By the 1980s Damone had fully rebounded. He now earns $1 million a year from his nightclub act.

$ $ $

Dorothy Dandridge
FIRST BLACK FEMALE TO RECEIVE AN OSCAR' NOMINATION

Dorothy Dandridge was the first black woman awarded the Academy Award for Best Actress. In the late 1940s and early 1950s she commanded a six-figure salary and lived in a Hollywood mansion. By 1960, her popularity vanished and she couldn't get work.

Then she married Jack Denison, a restaurant owner. As Otto Preminger put it: "She married that man, and they spent all her money. She had to sell her house and everything of value she owned. Then he left her."

Dandridge filed for bankruptcy in 1963. The petition listed 77 creditors with $130,000 in debts and assets of $5,000. She died of a drug overdose two years later with $2.15 in her checking account.

$ $ $

Eddie Fisher

1950's MUSIC SUPERSTAR

A Jewish kid from Philadelphia, Eddie Fisher owned the charts before Presley. But when the '60s came, Fisher's star sank like a rock. He blew his fortune drinking, gambling and snorting cocaine in copious amounts. Fisher's obligations eventually came to over $1 million. His debts included two lawsuits, then pending for $350,000 each. One was a breach-of-contract suit brought by Ketti Fings for an alleged commitment to coauthor an autobiography. The second suit was brought by a real estate broker who alleged that Fisher reneged on a house purchase. Fisher lost his home and all his personal property. He declared bankruptcy in 1972.

$$$

Mick Fleetwood
LEAD SINGER OF FLEETWOOD MAC

Mick Fleetwood filed for bankruptcy in 1984 in California. Fleetwood lost money in Australian real estate and an oil and gas drilling business. His assets when he filed were about $2.4 million and his debts exceeded $3.5 million.

$$$

Stephen Foster
COMPOSED "OH SUSANNA"

The great American folksong writer, Stephen Foster, wrote "Swanne River," "My Old Kentucky Home," "Jeannie With the Light Brown Hair," and most famously, "Oh Susanna." Forster sold his songs outright for a pittance to local music-publishing houses, often to feed his alcohol addiction.

He died penniless in a New York Bowery flophouse begging for one last drink. His royalties alone would today be worth countless millions.

$ $ $

Marvin Gaye

AMERICAN SINGER

Most famous for his 1970 hit album *What's Going On*, Marvin Gaye went into a downward spiral after his 1973 hit single "Let's Get It On." The singer divorced his first wife, remarried and filed for bankruptcy. Apparently, not all his tax debts were discharged, since pressure from the IRS caused him to leave the country in 1982. He rebounded with the megahit "Sexual Healing" in 1983.

Gaye died in 1984 after being shot by his father during a family argument.

$ $ $

Andy Gibb

1970'S ROCK STAR

Andrew Roy Gibb joined his older brothers' rock group The Bee Gee's as a mere teenager. The singer became an overnight teenage heartthrob. Between May 1977 and April 1978, he charted three No. 1 songs in a row. By 1981, he had four gold records and one platinum record.

When his relationship with actress Victoria Principal blew up, the singer buried himself in cocaine.

The white powder soon wiped out Gibb's checking account. He

"It's time to stop bleeding and get on with my life."

—MC HAMMER ON WHY HE FILED FOR BANKRUPTCY

filed for personal bankruptcy in Miami, Florida, in 1987. He listed less than $50,000 in assets and more than $1 million in debts.

Gibbs died the next year of inflammatory heart virus. He was 30 years old.

$$$

Merle Haggard
COUNTRY SINGER

Merle Haggard has been in the music business for 35 years and has 41 No. 1 country songs on his resumé, including the classic "Mama Tried." Though he continued to churn out hits into the 1980s, Haggard spent more than $100 million on a disastrous resort investment, an antique-car collection, four marriages and divorces, and compulsive gambling. In 1993, he filed for Chapter 11 bankruptcy and sold a portion of his song catalog to Sony Tree Publishing to pay off debts.

$$$

MC Hammer
GRAMMY-WINNING RAPPER

Stanley Kirk Burrell, a.k.a. MC Hammer, sold 18 million copies of *Please Hammer Don't Hurt 'Em*. He won three Grammy Awards. He earned over $50 million in the 1990s. But in April 1996 he filed for bankruptcy listing debts of $13.7 million and assets of $9.6 million.

A textbook example of how the-money-will-never-run-out thinking will ruin you, Hammer bought a record studio, 17 cars, racehorses and an estate with its own bowling alleys. He traveled by private jet with a 70-person retinue, which he supported.

Hammer also paid lawyers to fight 24 lawsuits, from ex-lawyers suing for legal fees to musicians claiming copyright infringement. There were just too many pigs at the trough.

$$ $$

Isaac Hayes
Blues Superstar

Raised in near poverty by sharecropper grandparents in Covington, Tennessee, Isaac Hayes was the country's first black music superstar. His first album, *Hot Buttered Soul*, released in 1969, established him as a cultural icon.

Poor financial advice caused Hayes to file for bankruptcy in 1976. The court auctioned off his gold-plated limo, designer furs and monogrammed soap.

Hayes bounced back in the 1980s with TV and film roles and a New York-based talk show.

$ $ $

Dr. Hook, a.k.a. Ray Sawyer
COVER SUBJECT, ROLLING STONE MAGAZINE

"Dr. Hook" of the '70's rock band called Dr. Hook & the Medicine Show found fame with *The Cover of the Rolling Stone* and other hit songs. The band and Sawyer went bankrupt due to financial mismanagement in the late 1970s. Sawyer said, "[T]he bankruptcy court took everything away from us, even the 'Medicine Show' part of our name. The judge let me keep the name Dr. Hook, because, obviously, I am Dr. Hook."

After bankruptcy, the band's next album was called Bankrupt. While the group bounced back with disco hits like *When You're In Love With a Beautiful Woman*, it disbanded in 1983.

$ $ $

Ronald Isley
ROCK STAR

Rhythm and blues superstar Ronald Isley of the Isley Brothers rock band filed for bankruptcy relief in 1998 to deal with a $5 million tax bill.

The Bankruptcy Court auctioned a 200-song catalogue and an 87-foot yacht. Included in the song catalogue was the famous hit *Twist and Shout*. Also sold was a $6 million judgment Isley won in a

"Somebody was putting the cash away, and it wasn't us."

—DR. HOOK ON HIS BANKRUPTCY FILING

copyright suit against the singer Michael Bolton regarding Bolton's hit *Love is a Wonderful Thing*.

$$$

Latoya Jackson
SINGING STAR

Michael Jackson's sister and star in her own right, sought bankruptcy protection on July 18, 1995, in New York City. The Moulin Rouge, a Paris nightclub, got a judgment against the singer for $650,000, which prompted the bankruptcy. The nightclub successfully argued that Jackson wrongfully reneged on a six-month performance commitment in 1993.

Jackson claimed she had between $500,000 and $1 million in debts and only $50,000 in assets.

Her husband and agent, Jack Gordon, said that the club had put a lien on Jackson's music royalties, her nude video for Playboy, as well as income from future performances.

$$$

George Jones
COUNTRY MUSIC SUPERSTAR

The East Texas native and country music superstar filed for bankruptcy after his earnings went into the black hole of alcohol and cocaine addiction. His 1999 hit *Choices* brought Jones back to solvency.

$$$

Cindy Lauper

1980s ROCK STAR

Brooklyn native Cindy Lauper sold over three million records with her 1983 hit song *Girls Just Want to Have Fun*. Before that, she sang with Blue Angel, a rock band whose first LP in 1980 "went lead" according to Lauper.

She took a temp job working as a file clerk for Blue Angel's manager, Steve Massarsky, to pay off a personal loan. When Massarsky sued the band in 1981, Lauper filed for bankruptcy under Chapter 7.

She won a Grammy Award for Album of the Year four years later.

$$$

Jerry Lee Lewis

ROCK SUPERSTAR

Great Balls of Fire! Jerry Lee Lewis filed for bankruptcy in November 1988 after the IRS seized two cars and a jet ski to satisfy a $3 million tax debt. The petition, filed in Memphis, Tennessee, listed a $950,000 debt to the Whiskey River Club in Nashville; a $40,000 debt to Memphis lawyer Irving Salky; a $7,000 debt to nightclub owner Steve Cooper and a $118 debt to the Waldorf-Astoria.

Bankruptcy Judge William Brown refused to wipe out $1.6 million

"It went lead."

—CINDY LAUPER, ON THE SALES
OF HER FIRST ALBUM WITH
THE GROUP BLUE ANGEL, WHICH
LED TO HER BANKRUPTCY

in federal taxes because he ruled that the singer tried to stymie collection efforts by hiding assets.

The IRS raided Lewis's home in 1993. It took pianos, furniture and personal mementos and auctioned them to reduce the remaining debt.

Because of the IRS lien, Jerry Lee has not received any music royalties for over a decade.

$$ \$\,\$\,\$ $$

Meat Loaf
ROCK SUPERSTAR

Working out of shared quarters in New York's Ansonia Hotel with music writer Jim Steinmann, Meat Loaf created *Bat Out of Hell*. Rejected by 20 record companies, the album eventually sold two million copies its first year and sold over a million copies a year from 1977 to 1996, making it one of the all-time biggest-selling rock albums. Yet Meat Loaf, the album's creator (along with Jim Steinmann), received no royalties after 1980.

Reduced to living off of his credit card while waiting for royalties that never came, Meat Loaf filed for bankruptcy in 1983. He listed $768,000 in assets and $1.6 million in debts, including a $91,000 credit card bill.

"The Meat," as he likes to be called, has asserted that he is owed over $14 million in royalties that he claims should have been paid to him over the last two decades.

$$$

Willie Nelson
COUNTRY MUSIC SUPERSTAR

Nelson went broke when the IRS disallowed deductions and demanded $9 million in back taxes. When the IRS came to auction off his farm, no one bid at the auction—the singer was too well loved.

$$$

Wayne Newton
LAS VEGAS SUPERSTAR

Wayne Newton, the famous Las Vegas crooner, who makes an estimated $7 million a year and lives on a 50-acre estate complete with pet penguins, filed for Chapter 11 bankruptcy in August 1992.

Newton's money problems began with a resort investment in the Poconos, Pennsylvania. The singer had speculated that casino gambling was coming to Pennsylvania—gambling never came. The property failed to generate enough income to meet the monthly payments on its $7 million mortgage owed to the Northeastern Bank of Pennsylvania.

Newton also fell behind on his $32,000 monthly home mortgage payments. Immediately preceding Newton's bankruptcy filing, the First Western Savings Bank of Las Vegas had begun foreclosure

"We'd be working
in the studio and
then they'd say,
'You gotta look out
for the marshals, the
marshals are gonna
come in tonight and
grab the tapes.'"
—Tom Petty

proceedings to auction his $4 million mansion. Meanwhile, the IRS sent him a bill for $341,000 in back taxes. Newton was also tardy on a $14,000 debt owed to American Express. Newton's Reno, Nevada, filing eventually listed 200 creditors owed a total of $20 million. He estimated his assets at between $1 and $10 million.

As of this writing, the King of Las Vegas is out of bankruptcy after having confirmed a Chapter 11 plan with the Las Vegas bankruptcy court.

$$\$\,\$\,\$$

Tom Petty
1970's ROCK STAR

Tom Petty of *Tom Petty and the Heartbreakers* got into a legal hassle with MCA Records after that company bought Shelter Records, Petty's distributor. Petty insisted that the sale canceled his liability but MCA sued him for breach of contract.

Half a million dollars in debt, Petty filed for bankruptcy in 1979. MCA's subsidiary, Backstreet Records, eventually inked a new contract with Petty worth a reported $3 million.

$$$

Run DMC

AMERICAN RAP GROUP

Despite over $10 million in gross revenue, rap group *Run DMC* filed for Chapter 11 bankruptcy in 1993. They filed to reject an early recording contract with Profile Records to secure a more lucrative contract.

$$$

TLC

1990's MUSIC GROUP

Rapper/singer Lisa "Left Eye" Lopez and her group TLC filed for Chapter 11 bankruptcy in 1995. Lopez earned her $1.3 million debt by setting fire to her boyfriend's house after an argument. The other TLC members—Tionne "T-Boz" Watkins and Rozanda "Chilli" Thomas—followed her into bankruptcy.

The group successfully used Chapter 11 to escape a highly unfavorable contract with their production company, Pebbitone Inc. TLC had enormous success with the quintuple-platinum album *Crazysexycool* but a pittance of the profits because of an early recording contract.

$ $ $

Richard Wagner
GERMAN COMPOSER

Richard Wagner was no starving artist prior to composing his operatic masterpieces in the 1860s and 1870s. Wagner had tenure as a conductor at the opera house in Riga, Latvia, from 1837 through 1839. He couldn't stay out of debt, though. In 1839, Wagner was confronted by a sheriff, who tried to throw him into debtors' prison. The composer fled by moonlight to Prussia and then England. He later spent time in a Paris debtors' prison.

$ $ $

Dottie West
COUNTRY MUSIC STAR

Best known for her hit song, *Country Sunshine*, Dottie West trailblazed a path for female country music singers. Despite her huge past success, West's record sales plunged in the 1980s while her debts mushroomed to over $1 million.

Her 1990 bankruptcy filing listed a $703,000 mortgage, $110,000 owed to a former manager and back federal taxes. The IRS held an auction of her personal belongings under a tent during the June 1991 Country Music Fan Fair.

$ $ $

Tammy Wynette
AMERICAN COUNTRY SUPERSTAR

Tammy Wynette, "the first lady of country music," sold more than 30 million records and won three Grammy Awards. The former beautician broke into music by singing in the Grand Ole Opry in Nashville. Wynette's first big hit was *Stand By Your Man*.

The 1980s saw a slump in record sales and bad investments in two Florida shopping centers. Wynette filed Chapter 11 in 1988 after the IRS whacked her with a back-tax bill of $900,000.

ARTISTS & WRITERS

$$$

John James Audubon
MASTER WILDLIFE PAINTER

The bastard son of a French sailor and his Haitian mistress, Audubon was sent to America in 1803 to run his father's estate, Mill Grove, near Pennsylvania. A natural salesman, he convinced his father's French friends to finance a Pennsylvanian lead mine. It failed. He then talked his backers into financing trading posts in Kentucky and then Ohio. Both stores went broke.

Needing fresh venture capital, Audubon pitched, of all people, John Keats, the poet, and Keats's brother. The Keats brothers sent him most of their capital. Audubon later claimed he used the Keats' money to buy an old steamboat and resell it to a New Orleans native named William Bowen. Bowen alleged that Audubon took Bowen's money but failed to deliver the boat. Some say that Audubon never even bought the boat and pocketed both Bowen's and the Keats' money. Undisputed is that everybody lost all his money. (The poet later described Audubon as "a dishonest man.")

The sheriff threw Audubon into debtors' prison. He emerged into sunlight after six months, upon an oath that he had no property buried anywhere.

Audubon left jail and lit out to the wilds of Louisiana to draw and classify birds. Although he failed to sell his drawings in America, a later sales trip to England proved wildly successful.

Audubon died in 1851, famous and well off on his 35-acre Manhattan estate overlooking the Hudson River.

$$\$\ \$\ \$$

Richard Bach
Mega-Best-Selling Author

Richard Bach's 1977 book, *Jonathan Livingston Seagull*, sold an estimated 30 million copies in three dozen languages. (Bach, an experienced pilot, had started writing the story of flight from a seagull's point of view in 1959.) The book earned him millions in royalties. Bach lost every penny by "investing" the money in an ill-advised commodity-trading scheme. Broke, Bach ended up living in a trailer.

The writer made a stunning comeback after marrying his second wife, Leslie. Together they wrote two bestsellers, The Bridge Across Forever and One.

Bach is alive and well and flying paragliders near Seattle, Washington.

"I was not anywhere near ready to live the consequences of the commercial success....[I] did what many did, found a friend and said, 'You handle this.'"

—RICHARD BACH, AUTHOR OF JONATHAN LIVINGSTON SEAGULL, ON LOSING HIS MONEY

$$$

Honoré de Balzac
FRENCH WRITER

Honoré de Balzac, who wrote, "behind every great fortune there is a crime," was, reasoning backwards, no criminal. The author of The Human Comedy and other masterpieces bought a printing house that failed in 1822. Since France had no bankruptcy laws then, the resulting debt—about $1 million in today's currency—plagued the writer for the rest of his life.

$$$

Lionel Bart
CREATOR OF MUSICAL OLIVER!

A Tony Award-winner, Bart created the musical *Oliver!* based on Charles Dickens' 1838 novel, *Oliver Twist*. The original London performance ran for 2,618 performances and became one of the most successful musicals in English history. *Oliver!* was made into a British movie in 1968. It won five Oscars, including Best Picture.

Bart sold the rights to *Oliver!* in the 1960s to finance a series of plays that bombed, including *Blitz* and *Maggie May*. Disappointment led to heavy drinking and drug use. Bart filed for bankruptcy in 1972.

$$$

L. Frank Baum
WROTE THE WIZARD OF OZ

L. Frank Baum published *The Wizard of Oz* in 1900, when he was 44 years old. His book was an immediate national hit, selling 10,000 copies in two weeks and 90,000 in its first year. Baum mounted an expensive traveling slide show and orchestra based on Oz, which failed to stir interest.

The show's closing led to Baum's bankruptcy in 1911. He died eight years later. Samuel Goldwyn eventually bought the movie rights for $40,000.

$$$

Matthew Brady
CIVIL WAR PHOTOGRAPHER

By the 1870s, the debts that Brady had incurred during the war caused him to file for bankruptcy. Brady pleaded with the U.S. War Department to buy the hundreds of priceless Civil War battlefields photographs. Uncle Sam wouldn't give him an answer. Meanwhile, while Brady was desperately trying to close a sale, his New York landlord evicted him because he owed $2,840 in back rent. The landlord auctioned off the contents of the photographer's apartments, including his huge collection of wartime plates. The winning bidder was, of course, the U.S. government.

$ $ $

Robert Burns
LEGENDARY SCOTTISH POET

Born to a poor tenant father in Ayrshire, Scotland, Robert Burns started writing poetry to escape manual labor. Although the author of *Auld Lang Syne* and *Red Red Rose* earned national fame after the publication of his first poetry collection, fortune failed to follow.

At age 37, the poet found himself in debtors' prison when he failed to pay for a new suit. Burns died of heart failure while raving about the tailor's bill. Over 100,000 people came to pay their respects at his funeral.

$ $ $

Raymond Carver
AMERICAN WRITER

Famed short story writer and poet Raymond Carver filed for bankruptcy in 1967, prior to publishing his first short story, *The Furious Season*. Carver gained fame and a job teaching at the University of California, Santa Cruz. But compulsive drinking interfered with his teaching and he resigned under pressure. He filed a second bankruptcy after losing that job. Carver finally gave up drink in 1977 after he met his second wife, Tess.

$ $ $

Miguel de Cervantes
WROTE DON QUIXOTE

In 1594, Miguel de Cervantes toiled as a tax collector for Spain's King Philip II. The king was preparing the great Armada to punish Protestant England. De Cervantes served as one of the many tax collectors the king hired to raise money for his navy.

After the writer collected some 7,400 reales in Andalusia for the crown, he deposited the money with a merchant called Simon Freire in Seville, in exchange for a receipt and a letter of credit to present to the merchant's bank in Madrid. When de Cervantes arrived in Madrid, the bank refused to cash the letter of credit. Freire had gone bankrupt and disappeared.

Having lost the king's tax revenue, de Cervantes was arrested and placed in a Seville debtors' prison. There de Cervantes dreamed up Don Quixote.

The book, written when de Cervantes was almost 60, became an instant, huge success, making de Cervantes internationally famous. The author paid off his debts in full by 1608.

$ $ $

John Cleland
AUTHOR OF FANNY HILL

John Cleland wrote the notorious *Fanny Hill; or, Memoirs of a Woman of Pleasure* while jailed in a London debtors' prison. In the early 1700s, Cleland served as a consul at Smyrna in Turkey and as a representative of the British East India Co. in Bombay. For unknown reasons, he lost his position and drifted in and out of British debtors' prisons.

It was to buy himself out of one of these prisons that Cleland wrote *Fanny Hill* in 1748. He sold the rights to the novel, an explicit sexual recounting of the adventures of a London prostitute, for 20 guineas. The book, which includes scenes of female masturbation, flagellation, homosexuality, group sex and sodomy, quickly became a major international blockbuster. It is still in print after 200 years.

Cleland was brought to trial on obscenity charges before the Privy Council. Instead of throwing him back in jail, the judge, one Lord Granville, awarded him a yearly stipend of £100 to continue writing, as long as he renounced pornography. Cleland lived happily ever after, becoming a respected journalist, playwright and amateur philologist.

Fanny Hill was universally banned until 1966, when the U.S. Supreme Court finally cleared it for publication. Nonetheless, the book is still being burned in Germany, England and Japan.

$ $ $

Samuel L. Clemens, a.k.a. Mark Twain

AUTHOR OF HUCKLEBERRY FINN

The son of a bankrupt Missouri lawyer, Samuel Langhorne Clemens bounced around in various jobs from steamboat piloting to mining. He later transformed himself into Mark Twain, lecturer, journalist and author. In 1870, he transformed himself again—this time into a very wealthy man—by marrying Olivia Langdon, the daughter of a New York coal mogul. The creator of Huck Finn and Tom Sawyer moved into a mansion with 19 rooms, 14 fireplaces and a 30-foot poolroom located in upperclass Hartford, Connecticut.

Twain's undoing came in the form of a high-tech typewriter called the Paige Typesetter. The machine could theoretically set type faster than any human. The problem was it seldom actually worked. Clemens put a total of $190,000 into the wacky gizmo, borrowing heavily to keep it going.

The bottom fell out in 1891 when it became clear the machine would never work. Hounded by creditors, the Clemens family escaped to Europe where they remained for nearly nine years. On April 18, 1864, Clemens came back to the States to file a personal bankruptcy petition.

He gave up all his assets, including his publishing business, and wiped out over $100,000 in debts. He was 60 years old.

Clemens recouped his fortunes with a hugely successful world-

"There are two times in a man's life when he should not speculate: when he can't afford it, and when he can."

—*MARK TWAIN ON HIS FAILED BUSINESS SPECULATIONS, WHICH RESULTED IN BANKRUPTCY* wide lecturing tour. He also wrote the *The Tragedy of Pudd'nhead Wilson*, which sold well.

$$ \$ \, \$ \, \$ $$

Stephen Crane
AMERICAN AUTHOR

Stephen Crane wrote the international bestseller *The Red Badge of Courage* in 1895. After his initial success he married Cora Taylor, a former brothel proprietor and notorious wild party hostess. After marrying Taylor, Crane spent all his money, and then some, on extreme partying, alcohol and drugs. He died of tuberculosis at age 28, besieged by creditors.

$$ \$ \, \$ \, \$ $$

Daniel Defoe
AUTHOR OF ROBINSON CRUSOE

Long before writing *Robinson Crusoe*, Daniel Defoe toiled as a commodity trader in London. He bought beer, wine, tobacco and textiles from Portugal and America and resold them to fellow Englishmen. At that time, when maritime insurance was still in its infancy, trading by ship was a risky business because of pirates and sea storms.

Defoe took his first hit when a freak storm sunk several of his tobacco-laden ships. He lost the rest of his money in 1689, when a

French pirate took a ship in which he held a major interest.

Defoe then turned to quick-money schemes. After reading about fortunes being made by manufacturing perfume from cat glands, he borrowed £850 and bought 70 cats. (Creditors shut down that operation before production could commence.) Next, Defoe borrowed to buy into a sunken-treasure hunt. That venture collapsed amidst litigation among the shareholders.

Creditors finally lost patience with Defoe and had him declared bankrupt for the enormous amount of £17,000. The sheriff arrested him and threw the future writer into Fleet Prison on October 29, 1692.

Defoe got out six months later. Financially ruined, Defoe finally turned to writing to make a living. Even after *Robinson Crusoe* and *Moll Flanders* he remained in debt.

Defoe died of heart attack while hiding from a creditor in a London alleyway.

$ $ $

Henry Fielding
BRITISH AUTHOR

The author of *Tom Jones* spent a term in debtors' prison before becoming a successful journalist, magistrate and author.

$ $ $

Dashiell Hammet
AUTHOR OF SAM SPADE AND THE MALTESE FALCON

Samuel Dashiell Hammet started out as an operative in the Baltimore, Maryland, office of the Pinkerton Detective Agency. He took up writing after he was forced to resign from the Pinkertons due to tuberculosis.

From 1927 to 1930 Hammet wrote his most famous books: *The Dain Curse*, *The Maltese Falcon* and *The Glass Key*. He moved to Hollywood and wrote for MGM, where his novels were turned into a successful series of movies.

Hammet blew his movie-writing income on hookers, gambling and drinking binges. While drunk he sold the rights to his works for a mere $40,000. Hammet spent his last days hounded by the IRS for back taxes. He died bankrupt in 1961, living in the gatehouse of a friend's upstate New York country estate.

$ $ $

Washington Irving
WROTE RIP VAN WINKLE

Before he penned *The Legend of Sleepy Hollow* and *Rip Van Winkle*, Washington Irving had to face, in the 1830s, the bankruptcy of his England-based family business. He wrote that the "detestable ordeal of bankruptcy" was "vile and sordid and humiliated me to the dust."

In Irving's most famous story, Rip Van Winkle took a 20-year nap—from childhood to retirement. Maybe Irving was inspired by his first experience in the workaday business world.

$$ $ \, $ \, $ $$

Albert Lowry
GET-RICH-QUICK GURU

Albert Lowry penned *How You Can Become Financially Independent by Investing in Real Estate*. The book sold over 500,000 copies. His popularity peaked in 1979 when high interest rates caused desperate sellers to accept no-money-down offers. Inflation also helped most real estate to increase in value.

Lowry's downfall came with the tumble in the real estate prices after inflation died down. Lowry made poor investments in a health club, a restaurant and a movie. He also lost millions in real estate development in Lake Tahoe. He filed bankruptcy in 1987, listing as assets a checking account with $11.68 and three small parcels of land.

$$ $ \, $ \, $ $$

Molière
FRENCH PLAYWRIGHT

In his 20s, Molière opened a theater in Paris, which failed. In 1644, he was locked up in debtors' prison. Twelve years later his plays became hugely successful. He died wealthy and revered.

$$$

Charles Wilson Peale
PAINTED GEORGE WASHINGTON

Peale was said to be the only trained painter who lived in America during the American Revolution. He became famous for doing the most reliable image extant of President George Washington.

Peale started painting portraits only after his Virginia saddle and harness shop went bankrupt. Peale settled in Philadelphia after fleeing jail term in a Virginia debtors' prison.

$$$

Rembrandt van Rijn
LEGENDARY PAINTER

As great an artist as Rembrandt was, if he lived today, bankers might still shrink from lending him money. Enormously successful in his youth as a portrait painter, at middle age his arrogance and temper offended well-to-do clients. Borrowing huge sums from friends and patrons to float a bloated lifestyle, the great painter repaid only a small percentage of his debt. He filed for bankruptcy in 1653.

BARGAINS OFFERED AT
REMBRANDT'S BANKRUPTCY SALE:

4 catapults and longbows

60 "Indian guns"

a large quantity of marine plants

the skins of a lion and a lioness

a Japanese helmet

a statue of the Roman Emperor Augustus

$ $ $

Harold Robbins
Mega-Best-Selling Novelist

Robbins published over 20 books, which were translated into 32 languages and reportedly sold over 750 million copies. The author's first career involved trading sugar in the New York Commodities Exchange. Before age 20 he had made his first million. In 1939, Robbins went bankrupt. He had bought shiploads of sugar at $4.85 per hundred pounds. Before he could resell it, the Roosevelt administration froze the price at $4.65.

Robbins then moved to Hollywood where he landed work as an executive for Universal Pictures. He began writing novels in 1957 and became a multi-millionaire with bestsellers such as *Dreams Die First* and *The Dream Merchants*. Robbins died on October 15, 1997.

$ $ $

Jerry Seigel
Invented Superman

Jerry Siegel invented the Superman comic book hero in 1933, together with his childhood friend Joe Shuster, who did the artwork. But he hit a wall trying to pitch it to publishers. United Features Syndicate wrote back, "It's an immature piece of work, attractive because of its freshness and naïveté, but this is likely to wear off after the feature runs for a while." He supported himself by delivering groceries. Finally, *Detective Comics*, owned by Harry Donnenfeld, gambled on Superman in May 1938. The character caught on immediately.

DC, seeing the potential, offered Siegel and Shuster a take-it-or-leave-it check for $130 for all rights to the Superman character. They took it. By 1941, Superman appeared in over 300 newspapers, eventually making tens of millions for Donnenfeld. Siegel sued Detective Comics in 1946 for a fair share of the profits. The cartoonist ended up losing his job, spending a fortune on lawyers and receiving a negligible settlement. His partner, Joe Shuster, was reduced to working as an adult messenger boy in Manhattan. Siegel died virtually penniless in 1996.

$$$

Gilbert Stuart
PORTRAIT PAINTER

George Washington sat for three different Stuart portraits. A few years prior, Stuart had sat in a London debtors' prison. He made at least 100 copies of his Washington portraits, including the famous unfinished Athenaeum portrait, to repay creditors.

$ $ $

Felix de Weldon
SCULPTOR

The creator of the Iwo Jima Memorial, de Weldon filed for bankruptcy in 1993. He was unable to repay a $1.5 million loan borrowed to pay for his wife's treatment for Alzheimer's disease.

$ $ $

James McNeill Whistler
PAINTED WHISTLER'S MOTHER

When Whistler was reading at the Arts Club in London's Hanover Square, he came across an unfavorable review of his work. The author of the review, the famous art critic John Ruskin, referred to Whistler's art as tantamount to "flinging a pot of paint in the public's face." Whistler had his lawyer, Anderson Rose, serve Ruskin a summons for libel, demanding £1,000 plus the costs of bringing the action. He was so confidant of a quick victory that he began construction of a new home, which he called "the White House." He also spent the anticipated award on lavish parties for friends, accumulating substantial debts.

The lawsuit was repeatedly delayed due to Ruskin's ill health. Whistler's creditors started dragging him to court. On September 17, 1878, his contractor, B. E. Nightingale, sued him for an unpaid bill of

"The fact that he was able not merely to put me in prison for two years but to take me out for an afternoon and make me a public bankrupt was an extra refinement of pleasure that he had not expected."

—OSCAR WILDE ON A CREDITOR

£655. In the end, Ruskin never appeared. The jury found for Whistler but awarded only "one farthing" and no legal costs in damages.

Unable to pay the legal costs and other accumulated bills, Whistler was declared a bankrupt on May 9, 1878, with debts of £4,500. All his possessions, including a Chinese porcelain collection, his paintings and his home, were sold at auction to pay creditors.

Whistler made his comeback when the Fine Arts Society gave him a commission to paint in Venice directly after his bankruptcy. This era proved to be one of his most productive periods.

$ $ $

Stanford White
AMERICAN ARCHITECT

The Mickim, Mead and White partner was famous for compulsive overspending on European trips. He went broke after a fire destroyed his uninsured house and possessions. White died deeply in debt.

$ $ $

Oscar Wilde
BRITISH PLAYWRIGHT

After Oscar Wilde lost a dramatic libel action against the Marquees of Queensberry, the court awarded £677 in attorneys' fees to the victorious defendant. Unable to pay the sum, Wilde was declared bankrupt.

The first meeting of creditors before the Official Receiver in London took place on August 26, 1895. Wilde's accounts showed unsecured liabilities of £2,676 and partly secured debts of £915 for a total deficiency of £3,591.

$$$

Frank Lloyd Wright
LEGENDARY ARCHITECT

Frank Lloyd Wright was the twentieth century's most revered architect. By the time he was 44 he had built 135 buildings. Wright was also in debt for most of his career. A low point came in August 1922 when the architect, then in his mid-50s, saw his practice completely dry up. He took refuge in his home, Taliesin, a Wisconsin compound founded by his family in 1911. But bankruptcy forced Wright to sell his collection of Japanese prints. Taliesin itself was then lost to foreclosure, and the great architect was unceremoniously thrown into the street.

The next decade would see him bounce back with his most acclaimed designs: Fallingwater in Fayette County, Pennsylvania, and much later, the Guggenheim Museum.

ACTORS

$$$

John Barrymore
1930s MOVIE STAR

This legendary actor of the 1930s lost all his money on alcohol-fueled parties and four expensive divorces.

$$$

Kim Basinger
9 1/2 WEEKS STAR

Hollywood producer Samuel Goldwyn once said that an oral contract is not worth the paper it's written on. Actress Kim Basinger discovered otherwise when she lost an $8.5 million lawsuit for breaking an oral contract to appear in the film Boxing Helena. Basinger filed

If it isn't the sheriff, it's the finance company: I've got more attachments on me than a vacuum cleaner.

—JOHN BARRYMORE

for bankruptcy to halt the loss of her home and personal possessions. Best known for her starring roles in *9 1/2 Weeks, Batman and The Getaway*, the sultry blonde star was the middle daughter of a loan-office manager father and ex-model mother.

In 1988, Jennifer Lynch, daughter of director Peter Lynch (*The Silence of the Lambs*), approached Basinger with a script treatment on behalf of Main Line Pictures, a fledgling independent production house. The story centered on a surgeon who becomes so obsessed with a woman that he hacks off her arms and legs so he can hold her hostage in a box.

After Lynch and an enthusiastic Basinger talked the script over, Basinger's attorneys drafted several "deal memos."

Having a change of heart, Basinger passed on the role on the advice of her agent, Guy McElwaine. Main Line sued her for breach of contract. In 1993, a jury in Los Angeles Superior Court found for Main Line in the amount of $8.5 million. Basinger filed for bankruptcy the same day so she could appeal the judgment without posting a huge bond.

The actress's bankruptcy filing revealed $43,000, in monthly expenses, including $6,100 monthly for clothes and $7,000 for "pet care and other personal expenses." Liabilities included $9,000 in monthly alimony payments to ex-husband, makeup artist Ron Britton, and a $900,000 note she signed to an investment group that purchased the town of Braselton, Georgia, in 1989.

The Main Line judgment was reversed on September 22, 1994, by the California Court of Appeals. *Boxing Helena* was released in 1994 starring Sherilyn Fenn and bombed.

$ $ $

Lorraine Bracco
GOODFELLAS STAR

Bracco filed for bankruptcy after a six-year custody battle with Harvey Keitel used up her savings. Bracco, the star of *Goodfellas*, *Someone to Watch Over Me* and the HBO series *The Sopranos*, said she filed after spending almost $2 million on lawyers while fighting to retain custody of her daughter, Stella.

$ $ $

Gary Burghoff
MASH STAR

Famous for his role as "Radar" in MASH, Gary Burghoff decided to quit acting after seven years on the popular TV series. The loss in income caused Burghoff to file a bankruptcy petition in 1991. The diminutive actor today sells his drawings of wildlife for up to $25,000 each. In 1999, he was touring with Neil Simon's *The Last of the Red Hot Lovers*.

$ $ $

Gary Coleman
1980'S DIFF'RENT STROKES STAR

When he starred in *Diff'rent Strokes*, Gary Coleman made $70,000 per episode and owned an $18 million estate.

The 4-foot-8-inch actor filed for bankruptcy in August 1999. Coleman blames himself for the huge financial losses, but he also sued his parents in 1989 for alleged mismanagement of $1.3 million.

A 31-year-old Coleman was reduced to working as a car salesman and security guard at the time of his bankruptcy filing.

$ $ $

Doris Day
1950'S MOVIE STAR

Doris Day went broke when her second husband, Martin Melcher, lost all her money by entrusting it to attorney and money manager Jerome Rosenthal. The advisor lost over $20 million and was later disbarred. Day never declared bankruptcy. It took her 20 years to pay the debts off.

$ $ $

Redd Foxx

Superstar Comedian

Best known as the irascible junkyard owner with the scratchy voice in TV's *Sanford and Son*, Redd Foxx lived well. At one point he owned a mansion in Beverly Hills, a Rolls Royce and a fleet of other luxury cars. Pretty good for someone who, in his early days, slept under newspapers and worked as a dishwasher. (Malcolm X, in his autobiography, called him "the funniest dishwasher on Earth.")

Perhaps remembering his rough start, Foxx was generous with the down-and-out, often appearing gratis at prison shows and charity events.

He was less generous with the IRS. Although he made millions from *Sanford and Son*, which ran from 1972 to 1977, the IRS sued in 1983, claiming he owed back taxes in the amount of $2.9 million.

Foxx filed for Chapter 11 bankruptcy in February of 1983. He listed $2.1 million in assets and $2.5 million in liabilities. Eventually an agreement was worked out with the IRS, allowing Foxx to keep much of his personal property.

$ $ $

Zsa Zsa Gabor
TV "PERSONALITY"

Famous for her eight husbands, her love of luxury and omnipresence on TV talk shows, actress Zsa Zsa Gabor filed for bankruptcy under Chapter 11 in 1995. She and her husband, Prince Frederick von Anhalt, had been ordered to pay over $3 million for libeling the actress Elke Sommer.

Born in Hungary in 1919, Gabor was the middle child of three sisters. (The youngest was Eva Gabor of *Green Acres* fame.) Raised with great wealth, Zsa Zsa received her first mink coat and 10-carat diamond as a gift from her father. "We all vent to schools in Lausanne, Switzerland," she has been quoted as saying. "I vent to veenishing school and even took vencing!" At 14, she was Miss Hungary. At 15, she married the ambassador to Turkey.

After her first marriage dissolved, she moved to Los Angeles. Gabor starred in Picture Mommy Dead, Queen from Outer Space and a dozen other pictures. Usually, she played rich blonde bombshells like herself. The Hollywood Foreign Press Association voted her most glamorous actress five years running. In 1951, she began her TV talk show career as America's own glamour queen.

Gabor's eight husbands have included Texas billionaire Conrad Hilton ("masterful and well-endowed"), with whom she had her only child, daughter Francesca, and Jack Ryan, the inventor of the Barbie Doll. Her current marriage to Prince Frederick von Anhalt, Duke of

Saxony, makes her a German princess. The duke, who obtained his title when he was adopted by the 81-year-old Princess Marie-Auguste von Anhalt of Germany, generates income by selling knighthoods for $50,000 apiece.

The actress's financial troubles began when she told Fretzeit Review, a German women's magazine, that Elke Sommer was broke, earned her living knitting sweaters and hung out in sleazy bars.

In 1993, a Santa Monica Superior Court jury awarded Sommer $3.3 million for damage to her reputation after the '60s sex kitten complained about lack of sleep and headaches. Regarding Sommer's testimony on the witness stand, Gabor commented, "She was crying and saying she couldn't sleep for three years. I never knew Elke was such a good actress."

Gabor put her 21-acre horse ranch in Ventura County, north of Los Angeles, on the market at $1.45 million. Her other assets included a mansion in Bel-Air and another property in Southern California.

Since her trial loss, resulting in the biggest libel judgment in history, Gabor has produced a half-hour exercise video called It's Simple, Darling. The video shows the actress in low-stress exercises such as slowly sitting and standing up. Between exercises, Gabor gives advice such as: "Girls, never forget when you break off your engagement, you must give back the ring—but keep the stone."

Maybe she knew that diamond engagement rings are exempt from creditors in bankruptcy cases.

$ $ $

Judy Garland

1930's AND 1940's MOVIE STAR

Judy Garland earned over $8 million in her lifetime. The star of *The Wizard of Oz* was one of the biggest box office draws of all time. Over-spending, divorces and drug abuse lead to continual indebtedness.

Garland got a reputation for skipping on hotel bills. The Hotel St. Moritz in New York impounded her clothing and barred her from the place because of $1800 in unpaid bills.

The actress died in 1969 of a drug overdose in the Belgravia District of London with over $4 million in debts.

$ $ $

Sherman Hemsley

1980's TV STAR

Sherman Hemsley became well known as the star of the popular TV show *The Jeffersons*. He filed for bankruptcy when a big investment with a movie distributor soured. Hemsley won over $1 million against the distributor but never collected.

$ $ $

Betty Hutton
1940's MOVIE STAR

Perhaps best known for her starring role as a high-wire artist in Cecil B. DeMille's *The Greatest Show on Earth*, Betty Hutton became a top box office draw of the 1940s. She earned over $10 million as a movie star but spent even more on an expensive lifestyle.

Hutton filed for personal bankruptcy in 1967. She spent her last years as a cook and housekeeper in a Rhode Island rectory until a brief Broadway comeback in the 1970s.

$ $ $

Grace Jones
POP SINGER AND ACTRESS

It is well known that cocaine is God's way of telling you that you have too much money. Cocaine will also help you rectify that situation rather quickly. A good example is Grace Jones. Jones became famous in the 1970s as a singer and played a villain in the James Bond film, *A View to a Kill*. Jones was arrested in the mid-1980s for possession of cocaine.

While she was in a rehab recovering from her addiction, one of her accountants absconded overseas with half of everything she had.

In her bankruptcy petition, filed in 1992, Jones listed assets of

$338,000 and liabilities of $1.6 million, of which approximately $1 million was owed to taxing authorities.

$ $ $

Buster Keaton
COMIC GENIUS

Buster Keaton, one of the great clowns of the silent screen, made an enormous $3,500 a week in the 1920s. When the talkies came out he lost his audience.

In 1934, Keaton filed for bankruptcy. He listed assets of $12,000 and liabilities of $303,832. In the 1950s, British TV started a Buster Keaton revival and in 1956, Paramount paid him $50,000 for the rights to the Keaton Story. He lived comfortably until his death in 1966.

$ $ $

Margot Kidder
TV AND MOVIE ACTRESS

Margot Kidder played the reporter "Lois Lane" in the 1977 hit movie *Superman*. She filed for personal bankruptcy after a freak 1990 car accident in her 1961 Rambler left her partially paralyzed. She had been working in Vancouver, British Columbia on the set of the *Nancy Drew and Daughter* TV show. When her car went out of control, Kidder suffered spinal damage. She sued the producer of the series,

Nelvana, for $1 million but never collected. Worse, by initiating a private lawsuit she lost Workers' Compensation protection under Canadian law.

Kidder also lost money on an alcohol addiction and by financing a doomed film production of Margaret Atwood's 1976 novel, *Lady Oracle*. The film was never released.

$$$

Veronica Lake
1940's PIN-UP AND MOVIE STAR

Famous for her long blonde hair, Lake was Paramount Studios' most popular actress during World War II. But after 1942 she began a long decline into recurrent alcoholism. The actress showed up drunk on the set and fought with the film crew. Directors and actors eventually refused to work with her. She filed for bankruptcy after a series of failed films.

Rediscovered in 1962 working as a Manhattan barmaid, she made one last film, *Flesh Feast*, which flopped. She died in 1973.

$$$

Peter Lawford
1950's MOVIE STAR

The British-born Hollywood actor appeared in B movies of the '50s. He is best known, though, for being a member of the "Rat Pack"—

SUPERMAN RELATED "COINCIDENCES":

Pierre Spengler, the producer of the hit film Superman encountered severe financial problems.

The creators of the Superman comic strip-Jerry Siegel and Joe Shuster both died penniless.

Margot Kidder, who played "Lois Lane" in the film Superman filed for bankruptcy as a result of a freak car accident.

Lawford, Dean Martin, Sammy Davis, Jr. and Frank Sinatra; and for marrying John F. Kennedy's sister, Patricia Kennedy.

Lawford's downward spiral began when his friendship with Sinatra broke up. He took to drink. Within a few years his marriage had ended in divorce and his acting offers dried up. His last work was a cameo on the pilot for Fantasy Island.

He married three times. During his last betrothal he was reportedly so drunk he forgot that he was already married. Lawford died penniless in 1984.

His last wife, Patricia Seaton Lawford, reportedly paid for Lawford's burial-at-sea ceremony by selling the film rights to the National Enquirer.

$$ \$\,\$\,\$ $$

Jerry Lewis

1950's MOVIE STAR

Once the highest paid movie and TV star of the 1950s, Jerry Lewis hit bottom in the 1970s when he was ridiculed by the counterculture. After bookings disappeared, Lewis filed a Las Vegas bankruptcy.

At age 69, Lewis bounced back in the role of the Devil in the internationally acclaimed hit musical *Damn Yankees*.

$$$

Randy Quaid
AMERICAN ACTOR

Randy Quaid, actor Dennis Quaid's older brother, starred in *Independence Day* and other hits. He reportedly filed for bankruptcy in January 2000, immediately after filming, of all things, *The Debtors*, with Michael Cain.

$$$

Lynn Redgrave
OSCAR-WINNING ACTRESS

Redgrave, facing debts of over $600,000 stemming from a complicated litigation with Universal TV, filed for bankruptcy protection in 1994.

$$$

Burt Reynolds
TOUGH GUY 1980'S MOVIE STAR

The star of *Deliverance* and *Smokey and the Bandit*, Burt Reynolds was the highest paid actor in Hollywood from 1978 to 1982. Reynolds grew up the son of a West Palm Beach, Florida, sheriff. He started out as a stunt man, getting his first big break in Deliverance in 1972. He went on to star in over 12 major films. Reynolds bought a private jet, a helicopter and five mansions, and kept a stable of over 100 horses.

The actor lost everything after his manager, Sandy Simon, allegedly advised him and a country singer friend, Buddy Killen, to invest in Po' Folks, a country-style restaurant chain. Reynolds and his friend bought 30 restaurants in Texas, Louisiana and Florida. The restaurants were mismanaged and the food and service nose-dived after the purchases.

Trying to make up their losses, the friends invested in Daisy Diner, another chain. They lost another $12 to $15 million. To make things worse, Reynolds signed personally on the Daisy Diner restaurant leases, so he was sued personally when the restaurants defaulted.

Since he had signed a release absolving his business advisors of all responsibility, he had no malpractice claim.

Reynolds disastrous investments collided with professional and personal disappointments. After 1988, Reynolds starred in a series of flops such as Smokey and the Bandit 3, which tarnished his reputation. His divorce from actress Loni Anderson cost $15 million.

Reynolds filed for Chapter 11 bankruptcy in 1996 after being sued by CBS for repayment of a $3.7 million loan. He listed $6.65 million in assets and debts of $11.2 million. Besides CBS, he owed money to Creative Artists Agency, William Morris and International Creative Management. Reynolds also listed some humiliating personal debts such as $121,797 to his toupee designer, Ed Katz.

Determined to pay back all of his debts through a Chapter 11 plan, Reynolds has embarked on an impressive comeback campaign. Since his financial troubles began he has had starring roles in

Striptease with Demi Moore, *Citizen Ruth* with Laura Dern and the TV series *Evening Shade*.

$$ $$

Debbie Reynolds

1950's *MOVIE STAR*

There is a class of celebrities who go bankrupt not because of any wrong action on their part, but because of the betrayal or incompetence of trusted advisors. A leading member of that class is Debbie Reynolds, who lost her life savings by entrusting her money to an incompetent husband.

Reynolds grew up lower-middle class, the daughter of a carpenter in Los Angeles. Studio talent scouts scooped her up after seeing the blonde beauty win a Burbank beauty contest. After toiling for a few years in forgettable B films, Louis B. Mayer cast Reynolds opposite Gene Kelly in *Singing in the Rain*, a role that catapulted her into stardom.

Reynolds' second husband (her first was Eddie Fisher, who later filed for bankruptcy) was Harry Karl. A millionaire in his own right, Karl seemed like a safe bet. But Reynolds was unaware of his compulsive gambling addiction.

By the late 1970s, Karl had gambled away his entire $28 million fortune as well as Reynolds' $8 million nest egg. Reynolds quit the marriage in debt for several hundred thousand dollars. Reynolds never declared bankruptcy. She repaid creditors for over a decade.

$ $ $

Mickey Rooney

1950's MOVIE STAR

The popular movie and theater actor who starred with Elizabeth Taylor in National Velvet and most recently in Sugar Babies, filed Chapter 7 bankruptcy in 1986 to when he came up short on some tax obligations. He blamed the tax mess on bad advice. This was a second filing for Rooney, who also filed for bankruptcy in 1962.

Sports Stars

$ $ $

Bruce Berenyi
Baseball Star

Former Cincinnati Reds pitcher Berenyi filed for bankruptcy in 1991 after racking up debts of $316,000. He kept his expensive condominium in Florida. That state protects all homes of any value from attack by creditors.

$ $ $

Rocky Bleier
Football Star

The former Pittsburgh Steelers running back and star of four Super Bowls went Chapter 7 in 1997, apparently due to the fallout from a nasty divorce.

$$$

Bjorn Borg
SWEDISH TENNIS STAR

Bjorn Borg retired from tennis in 1983 after making $10 million a year for several years. He put almost all his money into a clothing design firm and lost nearly all of it. In 1990, Borg owed approximately $5.2 million. The Swedish government sold his Stockholm mansion to pay off debts.

$$$

Jack Clark
BASEBALL STAR

The Boston Red Sox designated hitter declared personal Chapter 11 bankruptcy in 1992, despite a three-year, $8.7 million contract with the Red Sox. Clark's money melted into a $2.4 million home and an 18-car collection, including a 1990 Ferrari worth $717,000 and three Mercedes Benzes, each costing over $100,000. Clark filed in Santa Ana, California, listing $6.7 million in debts.

$$$

Brad Cousino
FOOTBALL STAR

The former Cincinnati Bengals player filed bankruptcy in August 1993 to prevent the foreclosure on his apartment complex.

$$$

John D'Acquisto
BASEBALL STAR

The former San Diego Padres pitcher formed an investment company with attorney Thomas F. Goodman called Doubleday Trust. Allegations of irregularities at the firm lead to D'Acquisto's bankruptcy filing in 1995.

$$$

Robbin Earl
FOOTBALL STAR

The former Chicago Bear filed for bankruptcy in 1993.

$ $ $

Rollie Fingers
BASEBALL STAR

Former Padre relief pitcher Roland G. Fingers filed a bankruptcy in 1989, listing over $4.2 million in liabilities and $50,000 in assets.

$ $ $

Tony Gwynn
BASEBALL STAR

In 1987, the same year he earned $600,000 and hit .370, Tony Gwynn of the San Diego Padres filed for personal bankruptcy.

$ $ $

Dorothy Hamill
ICE-SKATING STAR

Olympic gold-medal winner and ice-skating legend Dorothy Hamill filed for bankruptcy in March 1996. Hamill's case started with her purchase of the near-bankrupt Ice Capades four years earlier. In her bankruptcy petition, Hamill blamed her estranged then-husband, Kenneth Forsythe, for the Ice Capades disaster as well as for other money-losing investments.

Running into debt isn't so bad. It's running into creditors that hurts.

—*UNKNOWN*

$ $ $

Tom House
BASEBALL STAR

A former major-league pitcher for eight seasons ending in 1978, Tom House filed for bankruptcy after losing $1.1 million in a clothes and sporting-goods store. House attributes his financial disaster to condition called Terminal Adolescence. The syndrome, recognized by the American Medical Association, involves an inability to mature. House has since earned a doctorate in psychology. His new career is counseling athletes to avoid the same mistakes he made.

$ $ $

Harmon Killebrew
BASEBALL STAR

Harmon Killebrew had 573 home runs and a Most Valuable Player award when he sought bankruptcy protection for his business in 1993.

$ $ $

Joe Louis
BOXING CHAMPION

Joe Louis made over $5 million in his 14-year boxing career. He lost all of it to a compulsive gambling addiction. He made his post-boxing career as a professional wrestler for grocery money. In 1956, the IRS found that he owed $1 million in back taxes and hounded him until his death.

$ $ $

Harvey Martin
FOOTBALL STAR

Harvey Martin was instrumental in the Dallas Cowboy's 1977 Super Bowl victory. A defensive lineman, in a 14-game season he totaled 85 tackles and 23 sacks. When the Cowboys beat Denver in that Super Bowl, Martin and Randy White were co-Most Valuable Players of the game. Martin invested his endorsement earnings in a Dallas nightclub he called Lucifer's, a barbecue restaurant called Smokey John's, and an El Paso restaurant named Rib Cage. He also bought three houses, a Jaguar and a Mercedes. With no time to watch the store, Martin's businesses quickly ran into trouble. Lucifer's suffered cash thefts, his real estate investments turned sour, the IRS audited Martin and demanded $250,000 in back taxes, banks began to call in loans, and legal fees snowballed. The final straw was getting fired from his sports casting job at Dallas' Channel 5 and getting laid off from football during the players' strike.

Martin filed for personal bankruptcy in December 1982, listing debts of $611,987, 145 creditors and 11 lawsuits filed against him.

$$$

Tony Martin
FOOTBALL STAR

The wide receiver who helped the Atlanta Falcons reach the Super Bowl in 1999 filed for bankruptcy protection in April 1999. A week after the Super Bowl, federal prosecutors indicted Martin on charges of money laundering for a childhood friend and alleged drug dealer Rickey Brown. Martin's creditors include Gemma Ramsour, a wealthy retired woman who allegedly lent the football star $1.6 million. Martin claimed that the signature on the promissory note was forged. Prestige Imports in Miami claimed that Martin owed them $52,800 for selling them an allegedly stolen Mercedes Benz 500 SL. Martin denied knowing it was stolen. Martin filed for bankruptcy weeks before he inked a new four-year, $14.5 million contract with the Miami Dolphins.

$$$

Lawrence McCutcheon
FOOTBALL STAR

McCutcheon, a former Rams running back, filed for bankruptcy in Atlanta in 1988.

$ $ $

Denny McLain
BASEBALL STAR

Denny McLain, the Detroit Tigers star pitcher, was the first pitcher to win 30 or more games since Dizzy Dean 34 years prior. In 1969, he owned his second Cy Young Award as the best pitcher in the American League.

McLain got involved with underworld figures, which proved his undoing. He was suspended from baseball in 1970 for being a bookmaker and carrying an unregistered gun.

That same year he filed for bankruptcy with over $446,000 in debt. His major-league days over, he tried for quick money and ended up spending 29 months in the United Penitentiary in Atlanta for racketeering, extortion and cocaine possession with intent to distribute.

$ $ $

Craig Morton
FOOTBALL STAR

Morton, a former Denver Broncos quarterback, filed bankruptcy twice. He lost his money investing in a restaurant, real estate and South American hospital beds.

$ $ $

Craig Nettles
BASEBALL STAR

Nettles filed for bankruptcy in 1988, before the beginning of his 21st, and final, Big League season.

$ $ $

John Niland
FOOTBALL STAR

A former All-Pro guard with the Dallas Cowboys, John Niland filed for bankruptcy in 1983. Niland blames the drugs and women that came with being a Dallas Cowboy in the mid 1980s.

$ $ $

Michael Nunn
BOXING CHAMPION

Former middleweight boxing champion Michael Nunn filed for personal bankruptcy in 1995, listing $4.6 million in debts and $647,575 in assets. Nunn, who hales from Davenport, Iowa, listed the IRS and former trainer Angelo Dundee among his creditors. Part of the motivation for the filing was undoubtedly to void a promotional contract with Don King.

$ $ $

Gaylord Perry
BASEBALL STAR

When he pitched for the Giants, Gaylord Perry won 314 games. At the point he retired, he was one of only 19 pitchers to reach or surpass the 300-victory level. Gaylord struck out more than 3,500 batters and won the Cy Young Award in both the American and National leagues. The hurler ran into financial trouble when his 400-acre eastern North Carolina farm failed due to low prices for corn and beans. Perry filed for bankruptcy listing $1.1 million in assets and debts of $1.2 million.

$ $ $

Reggie Roby
FOOTBALL STAR

Reggie Roby, the Washington Redskins punter, became the second-highest-paid punter in the National Football League when the 32-year-old athlete signed up with the Redskins in 1993 for $1.15 million. He filed for bankruptcy in Miami the same year, owing some $488,000. Roby's bankruptcy was caused in part by debts associated with the 6-foot-2-inch, 255-pound punter's cookie franchise, Reggie's Gourmet Cookies.

$$$

Art Schlichter
FOOTBALL STAR

The former Indianapolis Colts quarterback filed for bankruptcy in 1988 in Columbus, Ohio. He listed $1 million in debts and assets of $1,800.

$$$

Sugar Ray Seales
BOXING CHAMPION

Seales was the only American boxer to win a gold medal at the 1972 Olympic Games. He filed for bankruptcy in Tacoma, Washington, in March 1986. The fighter's eye was damaged during a match and necessitated seven operations. He listed $160,000 in unsecured debts.

$$$

Billy Sims
FOOTBALL STAR

Sims, a former Detroit Lions running back, filed for Chapter 7 bankruptcy relief in 1991.

$ $ $

Leon Spinks

BOXING CHAMPION

From the slums of St. Louis, Leon Spinks rose to became the heavy-weight champion of the world. Spinks won the Olympic gold medal for the U.S. in 1976. In 1978, he won the heavyweight champi-onship in a 15-round decision over Muhammad Ali in Las Vegas. It was Spinks's eighth professional bout. He was 23 years old.

Seven months later Ali reclaimed the crown in New Orleans. Spinks made various failed attempts at comebacks, including a 1985 loss to champion Larry Holmes. Spinks lost his estimated $4.5 mil-lion in prize money to an expensive 1982 divorce and high spending on mink coats and luxury cars. In 1985, a bank foreclosed on his $125,000 house in the Rosedale section of Detroit. All his posses-sions, including the championship belt he won from the Ali fight, were sold at a storage company auction.

In March 1986, Spinks filed a Chapter 7 bankruptcy case. He listed as assets a $500 wardrobe and an income of $1,600 from box-ing. The boxer's liabilities included an $85,000 loan from Monarch Boxing, Inc. and a $100,000 contingency fund for a lawsuit pending by a woman who claimed Spinks punched her in a bar.

"I made a lot of mistakes.
If I had someone to show
me the right thing to
do and work with me,
then maybe this wouldn't
have happened to me.
But I'd sooner live my life
than someone else's."

—LEON SPINKS

$ $ $

Roscoe Tanner
TENNIS STAR

Former tennis great Roscoe Tanner filed for bankruptcy in March 1998. The filing was the outgrowth of a paternity suit by a New Jersey woman, Constance Romano, who said she had an affair with Tanner in New York. Tanner denied being the father of Romano's daughter, Omega Anne. He denied even ever meeting Romano. But two DNA tests, in 1994 and 1997, established a 99 percent certainty that he is the girl's father.

The tennis ace claimed a negative net worth of $543,000 in his bankruptcy filing, despite alleged substantial real estate holdings on Lookout Mountain near his home in Rising Fawn, Georgia.

Tanner won over $1.7 million in prize money during his peak years.

$ $ $

Lawrence Taylor
GIANTS FOOTBALL STAR

John Madden called him "the best player in football." Lawrence Taylor was named All-Pro nine times. He was chosen for 10 consecutive Pro Bowls. When he won the National Football League's most valuable player award in 1986, he was the first defensive linebacker to win since 1976.

Reportedly, Taylor succumbed to an addiction to cocaine. He filed for Chapter 7 bankruptcy in 1998. Lawrence filed in Newark, New Jersey, to stave off a foreclosure proceeding on his $605,000 Upper Saddle River, N.J., home. Taylor was charged with possession of crack cocaine in Florida and checked into a New Jersey rehabilitation clinic prior to filing for bankruptcy.

$ $ $

Bryan Trottier
HOCKEY STAR

Bryan Trottier filed for Chapter 7 bankruptcy in 1994 as a result of poor investments in an office building and ice rink. He listed $9.5 million in debts and $141,000 in assets.

$ $ $

Johnny Unitas
FOOTBALL STAR

Former Baltimore Colts prize quarterback Johnny Unitas filed bankruptcy in 1991 after the city of Baltimore refused to pay an outstanding loan it had allegedly guaranteed for Unitas. The Pro Football Hall of Fame member filed for protection under Chapter 11. Unitas seemed to have a weakness for unusual money-losing investments that included Florida swampland, and a crab and catfish company. The last straw came when he invested $3.5 million in National Circuits, Inc., a Baltimore electronics company. The firm lost a ton of money. When Unitas and two partners sold out for about $1 million, they were left with $5.3 million in liabilities.

$ $ $

Rick Upchurch
FOOTBALL STAR

A receiver for the Denver Broncos, Rick Upchurch filed in Denver. He said he lost $210,000 on an investment in his fitness center. The NFL strike also cut into his income.

$ $ $

Danny White
FOOTBALL STAR

Former Dallas Cowboys and Arizona State quarterback White filed for personal bankruptcy in 1987 with almost $13 million in debts and $50,000 in assets. He blamed poor real estate investments.

$$$

John L. Williams

FOOTBALL STAR

John Williams, a former Seattle Seahawks running back, used his savings to speculate in the financial futures market, losing most of it.

INVENTORS

$$$

Alexander Bain
INVENTOR OF FAX MACHINE

Alexander Bain moved to London from extreme northern Scotland in 1811. While Bain's telegraph was superior to the popular Morse telegraph, Morse was able to obtain an injunction against its use based on patent violation.

Bain went broke paying patent lawyers. His invention eventually became the fax machine.

$ $ $

Marc Isambard Brunel
DESIGNED FIRST UNDERWATER TUNNEL AND FIRST MASS-PRODUCTION FACTORY

Brunel invented the first mass-production factory. The plant mass-produced shoes for British soldiers during the War of 1812. When the war ended, Brunel had too much inventory. When he could not pay trade creditors, he was thrown into debtors' prison.

$ $ $

Edmund Cartwright
INVENTED POWER LOOM

English clergyman Edmund Cartwright was visiting a cotton mill in 1784 when he came up with idea of applying machinery to weaving. In 1789, he patented world's first power loom. The idea was slow to catch on. Cartwright went bankrupt anyway in 1793. A decade later, the man who helped spark the Industrial Revolution was awarded £10,000 by a grateful government.

$ $ $

George Washington Gale Ferris

INVENTED FERRIS WHEEL

George Washington Gale Ferris demonstrated the first "Ferris wheel" at the 1893 World's Fair in Chicago. Ferris refused to license his invention but he also apparently failed to patent his invention. Competitors quickly manufactured knockoffs.

In an attempt to publicize his invention, Ferris started his own amusement park. The park went bankrupt. Ferris was forced to auction off his wheel. He filed personal bankruptcy in 1896. His wife left him, complaining that he was obsessed with the wheel. The inventor has been universally credited not only with the Ferris wheel but also with inspiring the modern amusement park.

$ $ $

Charles Goodyear

INVENTED USABLE RUBBER

Charles Goodyear became interested in rubber when the material had a sudden popular appeal in the early 1800s. People lost interest because anything made of rubber melted into ooze in summer and hardened like rock in winter. In 1834, when he was 34, Goodyear found himself locked up in a Philadelphia debtors' prison. While in his jail cell, Goodyear experimented with rubber. In 1839, after his release, Goodyear accidentally created weatherproof rubber by mixing rubber with sulphur and applying heat.

Ever the absent-minded inventor, Goodyear poorly protected his patent rights and made ill-advised royalty deals. He spent whatever income he received fighting patent pirates, often unsuccessfully. He died $200,000 in debt in 1860. His family, though, eventually received substantial royalty income. The inventor had no interest in the Goodyear Tire and Rubber Co., which was merely named in his honor.

$$$

Johann Gutenberg
INVENTED PRINTING PRESS

Johann Gutenberg invented a method of printing from movable type. This method of printing stayed in use, with refinements, until the twentieth century. Gutenberg was trained as a goldsmith. In 1446, he began a partnership with Johann Fust, who lent him the money to develop the machine. Nine years later Fust apparently sued to be repaid. Gutenberg settled by turning over all his rights to his invention as well as all his stock, including type and his unfinished work printing the bible.

After inventing what some say was the greatest invention of the Millennium, Gutenberg apparently died penniless in 1668.

$ $ $

James Harrison
INVENTED REFRIGERATOR

A Scottish journalist who moved to Australia, James Harrison patented an ether liquid-vapor compression fridge. The refrigerator used a compressor that forced a refrigerant gas through a condenser, where it cooled and liquefied. The liquid circulated through coils where it cooled the air before returning to vapor.

Harrison hoped to use his invention to preserve Europe-bound beef and mutton during shipping. He gambled every dime on a Norfolk ship equipped with his new refrigerator and 20 tons of meat. But the chemical tanks leaked during the voyage, contaminating the entire cargo. Harrison went into bankruptcy.

Eventually, of course, later voyages proved more successful and Harrison's refrigeration system gained wide acceptance.

$ $ $

Matthias Koops
INVENTED MODERN PAPER

The ancient Egyptians made paper from papyrus. Later, paper was made from linen and then from cotton rags. In was not until 1800 that Englishman Matthias Koops invented a process to make paper from wood. He invested in a large papermaking mill but went bankrupt due to the high cost of his paper. It took a few more decades before wood became a cheaper way to manufacture paper.

$$$

Kirkpatrick Macmillan
INVENTED BICYCLE

Born in Scotland and trained as a blacksmith, Kirkpatrick Macmillan first got the idea for the bicycle when he saw someone riding a hobbyhorse. He set out to design a machine that could be propelled without putting one's feet on the ground. In 1839, Kirkpatrick Macmillan designed the first pedal-driven velocipede, i.e., bicycle. As a publicity stunt, he road it 70 miles from Courthill to Glasgow. For his efforts he was fined five shillings for running into a small girl and causing her a slight injury.

He never patented the idea. Others began manufacturing the bicycle as the idea caught on. Macmillan eventually went bankrupt.

$$$

John "Doc" Pemberton
INVENTED RECIPE FOR COCA-COLA

John Stith Pemberton was known as "Doc" from the age of 18 in 1850, when he bought a temporary physician's license for $5 from the board of the Southern Botanico-Medical College in Macon, Georgia. Doc Pemberton made a living hawking quack nostrums to the ignorant, malnourished poor of the post-Civil War South. He ran a chain of retail and wholesale outlets for dubious medicines with names like "Gingerine" and "Queen Hair Dye." He also became famous for borrowing money and not paying it back. Frank Robinson, a Maine native, became his accountant and confidant.

In 1879, Pemberton became enamored of cocaine. The newly discovered narcotic was internationally touted as the new wonder drug. Pemberton invented Coca-Cola in 1886 by combining cocaine with an extract from the West African kola nut. By 1887, Pemberton's debts caught up with him. To stay out of bankruptcy, he sold two-thirds of the assets of Coca-Cola for $283.29 to Willis Venable, a restaurateur, and George Lowndes, a fellow huckster. Eventually, he transferred the remaining third to another druggist, Asa Chandler, in exchange for the canceling of an old debt of $550.

Pemberton died penniless on August 16, 1888.

$ $ $

Adolphe Sax
INVENTED SAXOPHONE

A Belgian maker of musical instruments, Adolphe Sax patented his invention of the saxophone in 1845. Since the saxophone is a blend of brass and woodwind instruments, manufacturers of those instruments sued Sax for allegedly ripping off their design features.

Sax was financially ruined by lawsuits brought against his patents by competitors. He died penniless in 1894. Litigation over his instruments continued many decades after his death.

$ $ $

Charles Stahlberg

INVENTED ALARM CLOCK

After Stahlberg filed for bankruptcy in 1887, a Chicago businessman bought the rights and started what would eventually be called Westclox, which now makes 36,000 alarm clocks a day.

$ $ $

Bruce Vorhauer

INVENTED CONTRACEPTIVE SPONGE

Bruce Vorhauer invented the *Today* contraceptive sponge. He had made millions from the invention but lost the money in other start-up businesses. He filed for bankruptcy in 1990. The investor committed suicide in his island mansion on Salmon Lake, Missoula, Montana, in 1992.

MOGULS

$$$

P. T. Barnum

FOUNDED BARNUM & BAILEY CIRCUS

The Master Showman of the 1800s started out as a newspaper publisher in his hometown of Bethel, Connecticut. In 1832, Barnum accused a church deacon of usury, was sued successfully for libel and did 60 days in prison. Two years later he moved to New York City. He started his career at promotion when he met Joice Heth, a diminutive elderly black woman. He billed Heth as the 161-year-old nurse to George Washington and then charged tickets to see her. In the 1880s he joined with James A. Bailey to form the Barnum & Bailey Circus.

Barnum made big loans to the New Haven, Connecticut-based Jerome Clock Co. He had hoped the company would relocate to Bridgeport, Connecticut, where Barnum was developing real estate and owned, with a partner, 174 acres. But the Jerome Clock Co. went bankrupt, dragging Barnum with it. Barnum had guaranteed over $450,000 in notes. By mid-January 1856 Barnum was in bankruptcy proceedings himself. Although Barnum had transferred some real estate to his wife and his brother, Philo, he was in serious trouble. "No man who has not passed through similar scenes can fully comprehend the misery which has been crowded into the last few months of my life," he moaned.

The disaster inspired Barnum to find God. In 1858, he began in London a new world lecture tour called *The Art of Money Getting* which stressed a spiritual angle. The tour was a huge success. But it was not until the end of the decade that Barnum was able to repay fully his creditors.

$$$

Melvin Belli
LEGENDARY INJURY LAWYER

Known as the King of Torts, Melvin Belli represented Mae West, Lee Harvey Oswald-killer Jack Ruby, Errol Flynn and the Rolling Stones, among others. The Olympian figure in legal circles pioneered personal injury law in the 1950s and 1960s.

Belli's famous combativeness caused both his success and his financial downfall. He married and divorced six times. His last divorce, from Triff Belli, whom he accused of having an affair with Zsa Zsa Gabor, cost some $15 million. Belli fought with his law partners and was sued by his five former law partners. He had dozens of malpractice suits filed against him—one resulted in a judgment over $3 million. The IRS claimed several hundred thousand dollars in back taxes. In one of his last cases, Belli advanced $5 million to doctors and witnesses in preparation for suing Dow Corning on behalf of breast implant plaintiffs. When Dow Corning filed for bankruptcy, Belli followed suit.

His bankruptcy filing listed 127 creditors and 31 lawsuits pending against him. Creditors ranged from record-storage firms and employment agencies to former and current employees. He died of unknown causes on July 9, 1996, within a year of the bankruptcy filing.

$$ $$

Peter Bogdonovitch
DIRECTED THE LAST PICTURE SHOW

Peter Bogdanovich drew accolades for directing *The Last Picture Show* and *What's Up Doc?* in the 1970s. In 1980, he started the production of *And They All Laughed*. The screwball comedy featured his new girlfriend, former Playboy Bunny Dorothy Stratton. After Stratton began an affair with the director, her estranged husband, Paul Snider, murdered her and killed himself.

The film failed at film festivals and on limited release. Backers Time-Life and 20th Century Fox refused further release. A deeply depressed Bogdonovitch bought the film for $5 million. The movie bombed, again.

International Creative Management sued the director to recover an alleged $100,000 loan. Bogdonovitch filed for Chapter 7 protection in 1985. Eventually, he wrote *Death of a Unicorn*, a memoir about his relationship with Stratton.

Bogdonovitch filed for bankruptcy again in 2000.

$$$

Alan Bond
AUSTRALIAN MEGA-TYCOON

Alan Bond became an Australian national hero when his yacht team captured the America's Cup in 1983. A former sign-painter, Bond built a multibillion-dollar empire consisting of brewing, media, and real estate businesses. Less than 10 years after his yachting victory, Bond was formally declared bankrupt by a federal court after he failed to repay $194 million arising from a personal guarantee he gave on a nickel-mining loan. The man who once paid $53.9 million for Vincent Van Gogh's Irises told the New South Wales Supreme Court that he had no assets besides $38,00 in three bank accounts. Rising interest rates and debts of over $6 billion resulted in forced sales of assets.

$$$

David Buick
FOUNDER OF BUICK MOTORS

Scottish born, David Buick developed the overhead valve engine in the early 1900s. In 1902, he started the Buick Manufacturing Co. on a $5,000 loan. Buick's emphasis on craftsmanship resulted in only three cars being built. On the verge of bankruptcy, Buick ceded control of the company to entrepreneur William Durant, who recognized the need for mass-production. Eventually, the firm was renamed the Buick Motor Co. and became the basis for General Motors, which, in turn, has grown into the world's biggest car producer. Buick's shares in GM were worth was an estimated $100 million. Unfortunately, Buick sold his interest in GM in 1921. He lost the proceeds on bad investments in California oil development and Florida real estate. He died broke and forgotten in 1929.

$ $ $

Michael Butler
PRODUCED MUSICAL HAIR

Michael Butler made between $7 million and $10 million on the hippie musical. He spent the money on other projects that did not succeed. He declared bankruptcy in 1991.

$ $ $

Robert Campeau
CANADIAN MEGA-TYCOON

At its height, Robert Campeau's Campeau Corp. owned 40 percent of the office space leased by the Canadian government and built 20 percent of the new houses in Ottawa for over two decades. It also

owned Allied Stores and Federated Department Stores, which oper-
ates Bloomingdale's, Jordan Marsh and Abraham & Straus chains.
The retail stores were apparently his undoing. After the chains filed
for bankruptcy, the National Bank of Canada called in a $160 mil-
lion loan secured by Campeau's stock. With the crash in Campeau
Corp.'s stock, the bankrupt mogul owed about $100 million and had
assets of only $35 million.

$ $ $

Francis Ford Coppola
DIRECTED THE GODFATHER

Since even a modest commercial movie costs at least $20 million, a
reasonable film director knows he must restrain his grander vision in
deference to the almighty dollar. No one could ever accuse film
director Francis Ford Coppola of being reasonable. The director of
The Godfather and *Apocalypse Now* spent the first half of his career
scorning studio "money men" for forcing adherence to budgets and
the second half paying back personal debts incurred by flouting his
own budgets. Overwhelmed by the $15 million debt fallout from
One from the Heart, Coppola filed for personal bankruptcy in 1983.

Born in 1950 to a flautist/composer father and an actress moth-
er, Coppola grew up in Great Neck, New York, surrounded by art,
opera and literature. In 1965, he switched from drama studies at
Hofstra University to graduate film work at the University of
Southern California. Coppola's first job was directing B films for
Roger Corman.

But it was as a screenwriter for Patton that Coppola found success. With his Patton screenwriting profits Coppola started the San Francisco-based Zoetrope Films, a studio devoted to independent filmmakers. Zoetrope's productions were kept afloat by loans from Paramount Pictures. In 1973, the studio threatened to call in the loans, which would destroy Zoetrope, unless Mr. Coppola would agree to grant it one small favor: direct the new picture the studio was producing called *The Godfather*. With Zoetrope facing eviction, it was an offer Coppola could not refuse. *The Godfather* surprised everyone by selling more tickets faster than any previous film in history. Godfather and The Godfather Part II eventually took in over $800 million.

Critics trumpeted Coppola as a genius. Next was *Apocalypse Now*, a critical and financial success but a personal disaster for Coppola. When production costs soared $15 million over budget, the press blamed Coppola, painting him as egotistical and irresponsible.

Wounded, Coppola again rolled the dice, personally borrowing $8.5 million from Canadian real estate mogul Jack Singer to finance *One from the Heart*. The film cost $30 million and grossed $636,000. Even worse for Coppola, the press wrote him off as a control freak since he directed from a trailer crammed with electronic equipment. When Singer sued to collect on his debt, Coppola filed for bankruptcy to protect his home from foreclosure. Coppola listed $21 million in assets and $28.9 million in liabilities. Among his assets was a Napa Valley winery valued at $10 million, an office building worth about $1.9 million and a cooperative apartment at the Sherry Netherland in Manhattan on the market for $2 million.

Unable to pay off Singer without losing his home, Coppola toiled as a hired-gun director on movies such as *Gardens of Stone* and *Peggy Sue Got Married*. But it was the *Godfather III* that finally put him in the black. The film grossed about $160 million worldwide (of which Coppola received 15 percent) and boosted the value of the other Godfather films.

$$$

Walt Disney
FOUNDED THE DISNEY CO.

Walt Disney called his first company Laugh-O-Grams. Disney had quit his job working as a commercial artist for a Kansas City advertising company called Film Ad to start making cartoon shorts. Laugh-O-Grams was financed by $15,000 from friends and family. His first customer was Pictorial Clubs, a New York-based distribution company, which ordered a series of cartoon shorts. The company sent Disney a check for $100 and promised $11,000 upon receipt of six cartoons. Pictorial Clubs went bankrupt without paying for the cartoons. Although Disney continued to struggle with some small work—one job involved making a cartoon to promote dental health—he eventually ran out of money. Disney went bankrupt in the autumn of 1922. Immediately afterwards he left Missouri for California. He had $40 in his pocket.

$ $ $

Colonel Edmund Drake
STARTED OIL INDUSTRY

A former railroad conductor, Colonel Edwin Laurentine Drake struck oil in Titusville, Pennsylvania, on August 27, 1859. Drake thought that drilling was the best way to extract oil from the grounds. He was universally scoffed at. But after oil burst out of his well, thousands came to drill holes all over Pennsylvania. The oil industry created billions in wealth for prospectors and even for whole countries. The man who started it all got nothing: Drake never found oil again and lost all his money trying. He also failed to patent his drilling invention. He died penniless in 1880.

$ $ $

Duke of Buckingham
BRITISH DUKE

Also known as Richard Plantagenet Temple Nugent Brydges Chandos Grenville, the duke went bankrupt in 1848 with about £1 million in debts. His estate, called Stowe House, and the vast art collection it contained, was auctioned off while the Duke of Buckingham fled England.

$ $ $

William Durant

CREATED GENERAL MOTORS CO.

On September 16, 1908, Durant incorporated General Motors of New Jersey with a capital of $2,000. Within 12 days he raised another $12.5 million. In quick succession he bought Buick in Flint, Michigan, Oldsmobile in Lansing, Michigan, Cadillac in Detroit and Pontiac in Oakland. By 1910, GM owned 22 percent of the total automotive industry. GM ran into financial trouble two years later and creditors ousted Durant from control. In 1920, a stock market crash caused a collapse in GM stock. Durant felt obliged to buy back the stock from friends he had convinced to invest in GM. These purchases decimated Durant's personal fortune. He rebuilt his fortune by founding Durant Motors. By 1927, he had amassed a $50 million fortune.

Durant was wiped for the second and final time by the crash of 1929. In addition to stock losses, his bank failed, owing him $402,000. Debts exceeding assets, Durant filed for bankruptcy in New York City in 1936. He owed $914,231 and claimed assets of $250.

$ $ $

James Folger

FOUNDED FOLGER'S COFFEE

James Folger started out selling coffee grinds to gold prospectors during the California Gold Rush during the 1840s. The post-Civil War depression ground coffee demand to a halt. Folger went bankrupt in 1865. Undeterred, Folger worked out a repayment plan with creditors rather than give up his business. It took 10 years for the coffee maker to pay off his debts in full.

$ $ $

Henry Ford
FOUNDED FORD MOTORS

Henry Ford's first attempt in the car business began as the Detroit Automobile Co. in 1899. He spent the $86,000 he had raised from backers building a dozen cars over two years. The business did poorly and went bust after the backers backed out. Ford again got backers for a new company. He left that firm because he wanted to build racing cars and the moneymen refused. His third company, the Ford Motor Co., got started with $28,000 in cash. The firm's checking account was down to $223.65 before people started lining up to buy the revolutionary Model A.

$ $ $

William Fox
FOUNDED 20TH CENTURY FOX FILM CORP.

William Fox became one of the world's first movie moguls when he bought his first Brooklyn nickelodeon in 1904. Eventually, he

"Nobody helped me with money. I had no guidance."

—GEORGE HUNTINGTON HARTFORD II
ON WHY HE LOST $90 MILLION

bought more and merged all the theaters into the Fox Film Co. in 1915. The company was forced into receivership after the 1929 stock market crash. Fox was forced out of his company in 1933 after an antitrust investigation. Fox, whose net worth exceeded $100 million in 1930, filed for bankruptcy six years later in Atlantic City. His bankruptcy schedules listed $100 in assets and over $9 million in debts. Compounding his problems, Fox attempted to bribe his bankruptcy judge, J. Warren Davis, by delivering him cash in a paper bag. A jury trial convicted Fox of bribery. The former mogul spent a year in federal prison at Lewisburg, Pennsylvania.

$$\$\$\$$$

Paul Galvin
FOUNDED MOTOROLA

The company Paul Galvin started was named after the first car radio that his former company Galvin Manufacturing distributed in 1929. Galvin's first product was a gadget that allowed a battery-powered radio to work off AC current. That enterprise went bust and was put up for auction by the local sheriff. But Galvin borrowed enough money to buy back some of his equipment at the auction. He then came up with the idea of making car radios, which eventually resulted in the hugely successful Motorola Corp.

$ $ $

Paulo Gucci
FASHION MOGUL

The grandson of Gucci founder Guccio Gucci, and chief designer of that company, Paulo Gucci led the leather goods manufacturer to global success in the 1970s and 1980s. After disputes with family members, he sold his interest in Gucci in 1987 for $45 million.

Paulo Gucci went on a huge spending spree that included a stable of horses and an expensive divorce. He filed for bankruptcy in 1993, listing over $90 million in debts. He died two years later before the bankruptcy case was concluded.

$ $ $

George Huntington Hartford II
A & P SUPERMARKET HEIR

George Huntington Hartford II, known as "Hunt," spent almost his entire $90 million family fortune on failed investments that included an art magazine called Show and a New York art museum. While yachting in the Bahamas, Hunt decided to buy Hog Island for $11 million. He renamed it Paradise Island and spent $17 million building hotels and casinos. But he fought with mainland authorities over bridge rights to the mainland and a gambling license. Hunt sold out. His vision panned out and Paradise Island is now a top vacation spot.

Had he held on he would have tripled his inheritance. Instead, he lost almost all of it. He filed for Chapter 11 in 1992 to discharge back taxes. He now lives crippled from past drug use in a creaky New York townhouse where he rarely leaves his iron-framed bed.

$$ $ $$

H. J. Heinz

FOUNDED HEINZ CO.

Of all the stories of entrepreneurs who rose from bankruptcy to greatness, none is more inspiring than that of Henry John Heinz, the founder H. J. Heinz & Co. Heinz grew a two-acre horseradish garden into one of the worlds largest food packagers, with sales of roughly $2 billion in 1996.

Born to a Pittsburgh brickmaker in 1844, Heinz developed a green thumb as a boy tending the family's two-acre garden. The tastiest bounty of that tiny garden was horseradish, a plant that Heinz's ancestors grew for centuries in the river valleys of Kallstadt in Bavaria. Young Heinz grew so much of the stuff that the family had him sell the extra quantities to neighbors. At young Heinz's suggestion, the family pre-grated the horseradish root and sold it at a premium. The Heinzes innovated by selling the grated horseradish in clear bottles so people could see what they were buying. At age 16, Heinz had four employees bottling three acres worth of horseradish. In 1869, he was selling enough horseradish to buy an office in Chicago as well as a team of horse and wagons.

Things turned sour for Heinz when he expanded into the pickle business. In 1875, he entered into a contract with an Illinois farm promising to buy all the cucumbers they grew for 60 cents a bushel. Beating 50-to-1 odds, the cucumber crop hit unheard of levels. Heinz took delivery of so many cucumbers that they blocked the entrance to his office. At the same time a financial panic swept the nation, shutting off credit and drying up sales. In 1875, Heinz was forced into bankruptcy. Evicted from his office and bereft of staff or supplies, Heinz almost despaired. He wrote in his diary: "No Christmas gifts to exchange. Sally seemed grieved, and cried....I wish no one such trials." Another entry sadly records: "Bought a cheap $16 horse....He is blind."

Heinz made his comeback by borrowing from his brothers and sisters who scraped together $3,000 in capital. Soon Heinz began selling a product that would keep him out of the red for good— Tomato Ketchup.

$ $ $

Conrad Hilton
FOUNDED HILTON HOTELS

The Great Depression of 1929 hit Conrad Hilton when he had just built eight Hilton Hotels in his home base of Texas. Hilton Hotels was at that time highly leveraged—particularly vulnerable to the business disaster that slowly overwhelmed Texas. Hilton worked furiously to reduce expenses. He eliminated room telephones. He ordered his staff to turn off every possible light bulb. But the Depression had killed off his main customer, the traveling salesman.

"No Christmas
gifts to exchange.
Sally seemed
grieved, and
cried.... I wish no
one such trials."

—H. J. HEINZ AT A LOW POINT

After losing one of his hotels, the Waco Hilton, the future mogul took a mortgage of $300,000 from the wealthy Moody family of Galveston. He put up all the hotels as security. He put all his personal funds into the business and borrowed against his life insurance policy in a desperate attempt to meet interest payments.

Business failed to improve. A North Carolina furniture company sued him for $178. He couldn't pay it. One of his bellboys offered to lend him $300 (his life's savings). Hilton was so broke that he took the loan since he had no money for groceries. Unable to pay rent on his home, he moved his family into one of the hotels.

The Moodys foreclosed on all of Hilton's properties. But the hotels continue to lose so much money that the Moodys offered to make Hilton manager (and one-third owner) to turn them around. Eventually, Hilton bought back all his hotels.

Hilton never filed personal bankruptcy. But he did avail himself of the federal law, 77B, which would eventually become Chapter 11 of the Bankruptcy Code.

$ $ $

James R. Hodges, Sr.
OIL TYCOON

A resident of North Little Rock, Arkansas, James R. Hodges filed the largest bankruptcy in Arkansas state history. His debts ballooned over $115 million.

$ $ $

Nelson Bunker Hunt

FORMERLY WORLD'S RICHEST MAN

When it comes to spendable cash, no private individual has ever made more or lost more of it than Nelson Bunker Hunt. In 1980, Nelson owned or controlled 60 million ounces of silver (one third of the world's annual supply) worth $14 billion, five million acres of real estate in places from Montana to New Zealand, 20,000 head of cattle, and businesses from pizza parlors to horse farms. By 1990, Nelson lost almost all of it in the biggest personal bankruptcy case ever filed.

As a billionaire, Nelson lived almost monkishly. He dressed in cheap suits that never fit quite right. He avoided swanky restaurants, preferring a couple of hamburgers, which he washed down with Coke. For entertainment he strolled from his sparsely furnished Dallas office to the Petroleum Club to trade war stories with cronies. When he had to travel on business, Nelson flew coach. He drove aging Cadillacs, often scrambling to find coins dropped between the well-worn cushions.

Nelson started buying silver in the 1970s as a hedge against inflation. He started small, Hunt-style, by buying "penny packs," lots of silver worth several hundred thousand dollars apiece. Silver rocketed from a low of $1.98 to $3 an ounce. Convinced of its investment value, Nelson started buying the shiny metal by the ton. When he ran out of cash he borrowed roughly $1.3 billion to buy more, putting up all his assets as collateral in what became a gargantuan double-or-nothing bet on the price of silver. Banks were happy to lend Nelson money since the collateral, especially the oil and land, was worth in 1970 about $2 billion, $700 million over what Nelson was borrowing.

In 1972, the price of silver, due largely to Nelson's huge demand-pressure on the market, soared to $50 an ounce from $1.98 just a year before. Ordinary people rushed to melt down family heirlooms, silver coins, jewelry, dishes and just about anything made of silver to cash in on the bonanza.

As the supply poured in, silver prices began to fall, triggering daily million dollar margin calls to Nelson and his brother, Lamar. (His younger brother had earlier joined Nelson's silver-buying spree). When Bache Halsey Stuart called on March 3, 1973, demanding overnight payment of $150 million, Nelson and his brother finally came up empty handed. Bache sold the Hunts' silver, collapsing the market. When the smoke cleared, the Hunts owed $1.5 billion on silver suddenly worth $200 million.

In the aftermath of what came to be called "Silver Thursday," silver traders who lost millions when prices collapsed sued the Hunts, alleging market manipulation. In 1988, the government of Peru won a $135 million judgment against the Hunts for illegally attempting to corner the silver market, a charge that Nelson always denied. Sensing trouble, the banks soon started calling for payment on their $1.5 billion in loans.

Not to worry. Nelson had $2 billion in collateral backing up the $1 billion loan. Right? Wrong. While Nelson fiddled with silver, the bottom fell out of the oil market, and subsequently, the Texas real

BIGGEST INDIVIDUAL BANKRUPTCY:

Nelson Bunker Hunt owed $1.2 billion when he filed for personal bankruptcy. He was, only seven years before, the world's richest man.

estate market. In the mid-1980s, oil fell from $15 a barrel to $5 a barrel. The crash in oil prices ruined the Texas real estate market. Land selling for $100 an acre in 1970 now fetched $2 an acre. Suddenly, the $2 billion in collateral securing loans of $1.5 billion was now worth only $1 billion. Nelson Bunker Hunt, once the world's wealthiest man, was broke.

In September 1988, cornered by the banks, the IRS, disgruntled silver speculators, and even the Peruvian government, he filed for Chapter 11 in Dallas. The bankruptcy court auctioned off the coin collection, the real estate and the oil wells. Nelson kept his home, personal belongings and his two aging Cadillacs.

For someone who lost a billion dollars, Nelson did not seem too upset. In fact, life has not changed that much. He still wears cheap suits and eats hamburgers. On a mid-week afternoon you can still find the former multi-billionaire at the Dallas Petroleum Club, a place where he can schmooze with people who understand ups and downs.

$$$

Bowie Kuhn
FORMER BASEBALL COMMISSIONER

When debts from the failure of his Manhattan law firm reached $100 million, Bowie Kuhn filed a Chapter 7 case in Florida. He was able to liquidate enough assets before bankruptcy to buy a multimillion-dollar home at the exclusive Marsh Landing Country Club in Ponte Verde, Florida. Because Florida law allows for an unlimited homestead exemption to protect a debtor's home from seizure by creditors, Kuhn kept the house and stiffed the creditors. Kuhn's case was one of a number of high-profile bankruptcy cases in Florida that sparked demands for bankruptcy reform in 1999.

$$ \$ \$ \$ $$

Roland Hussey Macy

FOUNDED MACY'S DEPARTMENT STORE

An interesting category of famous bankruptcies contains people who try and fail for years and later succeed beyond their wildest dreams. Such a person was Roland Hussey Macy, the founder of Macy's, the world's largest department store. Born to an old Nantucket, Massachusetts, family, Macy chose whaling over clerking in his father's magazine shop. In 1894, he shipped on the Emily Morgan, sailing as far as the Samoan Islands in search of whales. When he returned in 1854, after four years at sea, Macy married Louisa Heighten, and opened his first store, a ribbon and linen outlet. Evidently, ribbons were not in big demand, since he soon closed up shop. For a few months Macy tried clerking in his brother-in-law's dry goods shop. In 1849 he quit again, preferring to try his luck out west, drawn by the California gold rush. He set up shop once more, this time hawking provisions to miners. Again, Macy must have been disappointed since he quit again to head back east and open a third store in Haverhill, Massachusetts, with his brother, Robert. Macy settled in for a full two years. The Haverhill store stayed open for two years. In 1855, the former whaler's venture went belly up, paying creditors 20¢ to 25¢ on the dollar. The future merchant king's credit was ruined for the next 10 years. At 36-years-old Macy went south (this time literally) to New York City, where he opened a dry goods and stationery store, occupying a space 20 feet wide and 60 feet long at 14th Street and 6th Avenue in Manhattan. Unable to get credit, he obtained goods on consignment. The first day's sales total, recorded on October 28, 1858, was a disappointing $11.06. By the end of his first year, though, Macy sold about $90,000 worth of goods. Macy's eventually became the world's largest store.

$$$

Robert Maxwell
BRITISH MEDIA MOGUL

Born in Czechoslovakia in 1923, Robert Maxwell fought with British in World War II. By the 1980s, he had built a media empire that included the *Mirror Newspaper Group*, *Macmillan*, *Berlitz* and the *New York Daily News*. In 1991, Maxwell fell off his yacht while cruising near the Canary Islands. Within a week authorities announced that Maxwell had stolen hundreds of millions of dollars from his corporations' pension plans to fund his empire. The news created suspicion that he jumped or was pushed off the yacht. Maxwell's companies filed for bankruptcy. His son, Kevin, filed personal bankruptcy and was tried but acquitted on fraud charges.

"I have worked two years for Nothing. Damn. Damn. Damn. Damn."

—R.H. MACY WHEN A
NEW ENGLAND STORE WENT BANKRUPT
BEFORE STARTING MACY'S NEW YORK

$$$

J. R. McConnell
TEXAS MEGA-MOGUL

J. R. McConnell came to Houston in 1979 with nothing more than a 1968 Camaro. In eight years he built a real estate empire worth $500 million. He had a fleet of limousines, a private jet and two dozen replica Model A Fords. The collapse of the Houston real estate market tumbled McConnell's highly leveraged empire. Federal investigators claimed that the entrepreneur's business was based on obtaining fraudulent bank loans by bogus collateral. He was arrested in November 1986. McConnell, 41, killed himself in his jail cell by stripped off the end of an electrical cord and plugging the other end into a wall outlet.

$$$

Bruce McNall
SPORTS MOGUL

Bruce McNall amassed a multi-million dollar fortune that included the Los Angeles Kings professional hockey team. He was put into involuntary bankruptcy by three creditors to whom he owed about $162 million. McNall had made his fortune trading rare coins and stamps.

$ $ $

Marvin Mitchelson
LAWYER WHO INVENTED "PALIMONY"

California divorce lawyer Marvin Mitchelson invented palimony while representing actor Lee Marvin's girlfriend, Michelle Tiola Marvin. Mitchelson developed a reputation as the divorce lawyer to the stars. He represented Bianca Jagger against Mick Jagger, and the ex-wives of Chevy Chase and Rod Steiger. Marvin filed for personal bankruptcy in 1993 owing $4.5 million in debts. He was later tried and convicted for tax evasion.

$ $ $

William Morris
FOUNDED THE BRITISH MOTOR CORP.

The son of a farm hand, Morris built and sold bicycles in his teens until he began designing automobiles in 1903. In 1904, his garage went bankrupt. Morris was left with only his tools and a £50 debt. Nine years later he produced his first car, a Morris-Oxford, an 8.9 horsepower two-seater. In 1952, his firm became the British Motor Corp., the third-largest auto firm in the world.

$ $ $

Clint Murchison

TEXAS OIL MEGA-MOGUL AND FORMER OWNER OF THE DALLAS COWBOYS

In 1984, Forbes estimated Clint Murchison's net worth at $250 million. They were off by more than $250 million. Murchison was forced into Chapter 7 involuntary bankruptcy by three creditors. He converted the case to Chapter 11 in 1985, when the collapse of Texas real estate wiped out his highly leveraged empire.

$ $ $

James Cash "J. C." Penney

FOUNDED J. C. PENNEY DEPARTMENT STORE

A native of Missouri, James Cash Penney was born to a farmer in 1976. He moved to Denver, Colorado, for health reasons. Penny dumped his life savings into his first store, a modest butcher's shop. His biggest customer was the local hotel. As the story goes, the hotel chef promised Penney all hotel business in exchange for a kickback of one bottle of whiskey per week. A devout Christian, Penney refused to pay. His shop went bankrupt. Broke, Penney found a job clerking for a drapery shop. Eventually, he bought the drapery outfit and started expanding.

One of the first retailers to expand via chain stores and franchises, J. C. Penney eventually grew to over 1,100 major department stores and 2,600 drug stores.

$$$

Roy Raymond
FOUNDED VICTORIA'S SECRET

We men have Roy Raymond to thank for the age-old problem of how to buy sexy lingerie for our girlfriends or wives (or both) without dying of embarrassment. After slinking away after his first underwear purchase, Raymond decided to solve the problem by starting Victoria's Secret, a man-friendly lingerie store. Partially financed by a $40,000 loan from his parents, the first Victoria's Secret opened in the Stanford Shopping Center, about 35 miles north of San Francisco. Within a year, the company had $500,000 in sales.

But while the first store soon became five stores, Raymond had trouble with the accounting end of the business. Suppliers went unpaid. Raymond was unable to find the cash needed for expansion. In 1982, Raymond sold the store to The Limited, Inc. for some $4 million.

Happy ending? Wrong. Raymond shortly invested the money in another store called My Child's Destiny, which sold expensive toys. The business collapsed in 1986. Raymond filed for bankruptcy. He lost homes in San Francisco and Lake Tahoe, and his luxury cars. His wife left him. After several other business ventures, Raymond again contemplated bankruptcy to wipe out tax obligations of about

$100,000. Instead, he drove his 1993 Toyota onto the Golden Gate Bridge, stopped the car and jumped 275 feet to his death.

$ $ $

John Ringling
CO-FOUNDER OF THE RINGLING BROS. CIRCUS

Al, Otto, Alf, Charles and John Ringling founded the Ringling Bros. Circus. John Ringling, the brother who controlled the business after Charles Ringling's death in 1926, made $1 million per year in the 1920s. In 1929, he made the disastrous decision to borrow $2 million to buy up most of his competition.

After the stock market crash and the depression decimated the circus business, Ringling defaulted on a $200,000 principal and interest payment. The lenders got a lien on all his personal assets and 10 percent and control of the Ringling Bros. Circus. The agreement also gave the lenders, an outfit called the New York Investors, the right to sell Ringling's assets at any time. Ringling's personal art collection was quickly liquidated. His other assets were sold piecemeal. The great showman eventually ran out of cash for even basic expenses. He died in 1936, leaving an insolvent estate.

$ $ $

Charles Schwab
FOUNDED BETHLEHEM STEEL

Charles Schwab was one of the wealthiest men of his time. At the height of his career, Schwab's fortune amounted to $25 million. But by 1932, the market value of Schwab's 90,000 shares in Bethlehem Steel had fallen to $1,260,000. He turned over his mansion Riverside to the Chase National Bank to satisfy debts. Schwab moved into a small Manhattan apartment at 290 Park Avenue. When he died on September 19, 1939, his assets were $1,389,509 but his liabilities were $1,727,858—a deficit of over $300,000.

$ $ $

Morris Shenker
LAS VEGAS MOB LAWYER

Morris Shenker is best known for representing Jimmy Hoffa. He also represented more clients than any other attorney at the famous 1954 Kefauver hearings on organized crime. He filed Chapter 11 in 1984 to discharge a $64 million debt to the Department of Labor for pension fraud and an IRS claim for some $54 million.

$ $ $

Pierre Spengler
PRODUCED SUPERMAN MOVIES

Spengler produced the film series with Alexander and Ilya Salkind. The Superman films took in over $400 million at the box office. Spengler filed for personal bankruptcy in Britain.

$ $ $

Donald Trump
NEW YORK REAL ESTATE TYCOON

If you owe the bank a million dollars and you can't pay, you're in trouble. If you owe the bank a billion dollars and you can't pay, the bank's in trouble. Business Week estimated in 1992 that Donald Trump, the flamboyant New York developer, had at the time a negative net worth of almost $1.4 billion. Trump, known to his fans as "The Donald," showed true grace under pressure. While other moguls threw fits and filed for bankruptcy, Trump coolly convinced his creditors that he was worth more to them out of bankruptcy than in it. The lenders lowered his personal debt from $885 million to $115 million. Trump held onto major properties such as Trump Tower, his half-interest in the Plaza Hotel and undeveloped land along the Hudson River.

The real estate boom of the late 1990s found Trump back in top form with shiny new developments such as the Trump International Hotel and the construction of the world's tallest residential condominium near the United Nations.

$$$

John Walter
FOUNDED LONDON TIMES

Starting out as an insurer of the shipping trade, John Walter found himself underwater at age 43 when a Jamaican hurricane sank a ship he had insured. Walter went into publishing by buying a scandal sheet, turning it respectable and renaming it the London Times.

$$$

Sam Walton
FOUNDED WAL-MART

Sam Walton's first store was a Ben Franklin discount shop, which he made one of the most successful in the chain. But Walton made the mistake of signing a short lease. When his store became a success the landlord simply evicted Walton and took over the store. The future billionaire had to start from scratch in another state. After that experience, Walton encouraged his oldest son to go to law school.

$$$

Bill Zeckendorf

BUILT UNITED NATIONS

New York real estate developer William Zeckendorf helped build the United Nations complex. He filed for personal bankruptcy in 1968 as a result of personal loan guarantees to his defunct firm, Webb & Knapp.

$$$

Florenz Ziegfeld

LEGENDARY SHOWMAN

Florenz Ziegfeld, born in 1869 in Chicago, is best known for the Ziegfeld Follies, an elaborate Manhattan revue produced annually for 24 years. His other productions include Show Boat, in 1927, and Bitter Sweet, in 1929.

On the day the stock market crashed, October 29, 1929, Ziegfeld was in small claims court countersuing the Strauss Sign Co. regarding a faulty electric sign. His stockbrokers, led by Ed Hutton, who founded E.F. Hutton, frantically tried to reach him to get him to cut his losses. When Ziegfeld finally emerged from court he was completely ruined. He had bought $2 million in stocks on 90 percent margin. For the next two years he evaded process servers by leaving a side entrance of his famous 55th Street Theater. He died penniless in 1932.